Miss
Secret Ri

1916-1918

I dedicate this book to Louis,
The wind beneath my wings–

Matador
9 Priory Business Park,
Wistow Road, Kibworth Beauchamp,
Leicestershire. LE8 0RX
Tel: 0116 279 2299
Email: books@troubador.co.uk
Web: www.troubador.co.uk/matador
Twitter: @matadorbooks

ISBN PB: 978 1788033 176
HB: 978 1788036 832

British Library Cataloguing in Publication Data.
A catalogue record for this book is available from the British Library.

Printed and bound by CPI Group (UK) Ltd, Croydon, CR0 4YY
Typeset in 11pt Minion Pro by Troubador Publishing Ltd, Leicester, UK

Matador is an imprint of Troubador Publishing Ltd

Introduction

Miss Daisy, my mother, worked as an English governess in St Petersburg, Russia, from 1910 to the end of 1917. The last two years are recorded in her diary, a day-to-day account of her life and the families who employed her, before and during the First World War and the Revolution.

She and her two sisters were born in St Petersburg where their father, who had lived in Russia most of his life, was manager of an iron foundry employing over 500 men. They were fluent in the Russian language and lived a prosperous life. In 1904 as young children they were brought to Lancashire, their mother's birthplace, almost penniless after the first outbreak of the revolution when widespread strikes and violence closed down many of the big industrial firms and her father lost all his money invested in shares and insurance policies at the foundry.

In the years following 1910 the three sisters sailed out from Hull to St Petersburg or Petrograd as it became during the war, hoping for a better life, where all three were employed as English governesses. Their father, devastated by his loss, became an alcoholic so each sister sent one-third of their wages back home to their mother and with no particular interest in politics found themselves trapped in the mayhem and violence on the streets of Petrograd within the very dangerous environs of the Russian aristocracy during the 1917 revolution. The return journey to England became an impossible dream because they had not enough money to pay the fare.

The life of a governess in more peaceful times was a very

isolated existence, most of it spent in the nursery with only one afternoon a week off duty. There was no opportunity to make any friends their own age outside the family but changes made by the war and the revolution gave them a little more freedom. The diary slowly unfolds with the everyday preoccupations of her life, namely to protect the children, her sisters welfare, the young officer returning from the trenches to declare his love, her imprisonment and subsequent wanderings, amongst which appear some of the most infamous characters of those pre-revolutionary years – Rasputin, Anna Verubova, the Tsarina and her daughters, Lenin and Trotsky. No-one seemed to realise until it was too late that what was about to happen would change their lives completely, for some in the most brutal circumstances.

My mother and her sisters were among the last in a long line of highly esteemed English governesses to leave St Petersburg. They left behind those much-loved children and wealthy families who became some of the most impoverished, itinerant people scattered throughout Europe in a changed world they did not understand.

The diary was hidden away in a suitcase for most of her later life until it became part of my inheritance, along with letters and photographs. Throughout her long life she corresponded with her former employers, Natasha and Nina Michaelovna, often sitting up until well after midnight with a Russian grammar book, determined not to forget the language and after a gap of almost 50 years met them again on a trip to Leningrad in 1965. When at last she let me read the diary she just shook her head and said, 'Remember, we were all very young when I wrote that'.

Many years later when computers became a commonplace addition to the household, a friend introduced me to a website, 'Alexander Palace Time Machine', which lists books about the Russian revolution. In one of these, 'The Memoirs of Anna Verubova', the author, a close friend of the Tsarina Alexandra, quotes one of the last letters written from her captivity in Tobolsk in which she mentions 'Miss Ida', my mother's sister, who was governess to the three children of Anna Verubova's sister. With this startling discovery I decided to edit and publish my mother's diary, spending long hours with old photographs, letters and the diary where some of the names were written in code.

After the revolution, World War II and the siege of Leningrad, many of the streets, buildings and bridges were rebuilt and some renamed. I was lucky enough to find a 1916 'Baedecker Tourist Guide' to St Petersburg in which I was able to locate many of the places where the sisters lived, even finding where the old Phoenix Iron Foundry and house once stood in the Viborg district where they were born. Finally, on a trip to Russia I met my mother's employer Nina Michaelovna, a very old lady dressed in black, who held my hand throughout the entire visit, remembering things from so many long years ago. In Moscow I saw the embalmed body of Lenin. Lying in an ice-cold cellar, he was dressed in a dark suit with shiny, polished shoes like a puppet that had lost its strings. Two armed guards stood at his head and feet. Following a long queue of tourists, we moved slowly around the body from head to feet and around the other side with a last look at his face. Here lay the man who had once asked Ida, an English governess with a British passport, how it was that she spoke such good Russian.

It is now exactly 100 years since Miss Daisy sat with a scratchy pen nib and bottle of ink filling in her diary after midnight when everyone else was asleep, so this will be a centenary landmark and a memory of lost youth.

M. delaHaye
2016

NB: The rouble was worth approximately 10 roubles to the £1 up to 1917.

Acknowledgements – With many thanks to Gill Parry for her patience and work at the computer.

THE DIARY

Kristos Voskres! Christ is Risen! The old familiar greeting on Easter morning and bells ringing out but today has been such a long, weary drag. My pupils, Petya and Natasha are ill. Both have mumps. Our visits to church were cancelled and I have been confined to the house for the whole day with no fresh air, mainly reading stories to the children.

They gave me a very nice photo album for my Easter present and I got 30 roubles from my employers, also this linen-bound book which Nina Michaelovna, the children's mother, says I must keep as a diary but I wonder whether I will have the patience to write a full account every evening as the days are too much alike to prove interesting. The pages are blank, no dates, so I can write as much as I like. It will be in English, much harder for Nina Michaelovna to understand – must find a secret hiding place somewhere in my room.

I can hardly believe 6 years have passed in this way since I first started to work here as English governess to the Loukin family. It was in 1910 and I was just 17 years old. It seems so long ago. Six long years since I last saw my mother. Nina Michaelovna has become more like a mother than an employer. The children have grown up with me. Petya is 9 years old and Natasha is 7. Both were looking forward to Easter so much after the freezing winter but we did manage to paint and dye some eggs for the table which, in spite of everything, was laid out as usual with the artificial green grass and coloured eggs down the centre and plenty of *paska* and *kulich*[1] for visitors, even a big, round Easter cake with lots of icing.

I should say it is very difficult not to be religious in this household, with icons in almost every room and all the servants praying to a thousand saints whenever anything goes wrong. During Lent we are not supposed to eat any butter, cheese or eggs but I'm afraid we did because the children are so young. I certainly missed the excitement of early morning service when we all stand outside the church with candles until the priest arrives. He peers inside the empty church, then turns around to the crowd and in such a loud, triumphant voice calls out, '*Kristos Voskres!*' Christ is risen! and we, the congregation, reply with the words, '*Voistini Voskrese!*' Truly he is risen! It reminds me so much of my childhood and my mother and father. It is all a re-enactment of the discovery of Christ's tomb when the stone was rolled away. My father always told us, that should we meet the most awful, ragged-looking beggar near the church steps, we had to kiss him three times on the cheeks saying these same words. I miss my mother who is in England so much. She is so far away and since the war has been going on for two years we have no hope of travelling. I could not afford the fare to England anyway.

Nina Michaelovna Loukina is an Armenian and refuses to speak any English although she understands it well enough. She and her husband Piotr Petrovitch are both from military families. She is the daughter of a general. She has jet black hair and very dark, sparkling eyes, not pretty but very elegant and striking in appearance with a very straight back and statuesque shoulders and neck. You would never see her sink into a chair like me. He is a professor of engineering at the Admiralty, very strict and critical. Everything has to run smoothly in this

---

1   A kind of sweetbread with icing on top.

household or there is a big row. 'Rules are there to be followed and kept,' he used to say to me when I first came here. He adores Natasha and she is very spoilt by both parents.

When Nina Michaelovna is late home from visiting, my goodness, she does not show any haste or any signs of it. She just sits down at the piano very composed and plays something calm and beautiful. He has no idea that she has just rushed in through the door. Before she married she used to appear on the stage singing opera. She is very kind and generous as a rule but sometimes gets very cross if I forget to do anything she has told me. Nothing much escapes her attention. We all have to pull long faces when Piotr Petrovitch is around as he does not like to see any giggling or silly work which I do with the children. He prefers to talk about the war and we all have to be on our very best behaviour.

Quite late in the day Nina Michaelovna's four brothers arrived, all in military uniform except for Uncle Constantin, the eldest. They each presented me with a little silver Easter egg. Then an officer of the Guards dropped in to say goodbye before going off to the war and a lot of talking went on. She is at this moment going ninety to the dozen on the telephone. The poor officer must have felt talked to death as he left looking quite pale and distracted. I'm so glad someone else can beat me at talking. I will be very glad when the holiday is over. I don't like holidays very much as Piotr Petrovitch is in charge of everything when he is at home and very critical of everything we do, although my two sisters, also employed as English governesses, are allowed to visit and I to them.

11TH APRIL 1916 – MONDAY

I hate sitting in the house all day without any air. Unlike England most of the houses and apartments here in town have double windows and are heated by stoves and radiators which make the air very stuffy, so we are glad to get out for some fresh air however cold it is. Today Piotr Petrovitch has been promoted to Colonel of the First Ranks so raced off at once to get new epaulettes. Just now they are getting ready to go out visiting. This evening my eldest sister May called and with her was Mr Cummings, an English businessman, who recently proposed to her. He looked quite confused and nervous as this is the first time he has been to our house and all depends on May's answer whether he will ever come again. We were in the sitting room drinking tea, when Ida my other sister turned up. Since we all work as English governesses and have only one afternoon off during the whole week, we have a lot to talk about. At 11.00pm I accompanied them a little of the way home and now here I am scratching away at my new diary.

No wonder I never go to sleep before 1.00am or even later because it is the only time I have to myself without interruptions. I wonder what May will say to Mr Cummings? As a matter of fact, I can guess quite easily. Anyway she is off to Yaroslavl tomorrow with her family, the Sartissons, with whom she has lived for the past six years.

How on earth could she possibly leave them to marry a stranger, even if he is English? May is the luckiest one of the three of us. She is very happy in her place and has only one child to devote all her time to. They live in the most beautiful place you can imagine, the Podmener Estate in Terijoki, Finland, which is owned by Mrs Sartisson's father who is a Russian Jew. The gardens are full of exotic plants and trees where they say that even the soil was imported when it was first built. They are entirely self-sufficient as far as food is concerned. They have their own farm and employ a great many servants. Mr Sartisson is Swedish Russian, working as an engineering representative for Scandinavia. Every summer, that is until the war started in 1914, they went off travelling around Europe. Whilst in Paris, May would make the short journey over to England to see our mother. I still have a collection of postcards from Switzerland, the south of France and Baden Baden, in fact all the famous watering holes of Europe. Mr Sartisson would join them for a short time but mostly it was just May who helped Mrs Sartisson with her shopping and with Valentina, her daughter. They occupy almost every waking hour of May's life. Being a governess in what is popularly regarded as a very good job is not all it's cracked up to be in spite of being very well paid. Most of the time it is just monotonous and very boring nursery training. They employ tutors for children from the age of six or seven. I would say that May is most suited to the job since she was always curled up with a book when we were children, nicknamed 'bookworm' by our father, whilst I was known as a tom-boy, a live wire continually running about looking for some kind of excitement.

I thought May would be very lonely out there amongst the pine trees and birch forests of Finland but she is very contented, finds everything just as convenient as in town. The estate also houses Mrs Sartisson's two sisters, Vara and Sonia, her brother Felix and his wife, plus numerous visiting tutors for Valentina, known as Vava for short. They also have an apartment here in Petrograd so she is not as isolated as one might think. Vava is nine years old. Anyway, they are off to Yaroslavl tomorrow for the summer. Ida pointed out that it was rather a well timed journey. No, May will not be swept off her feet by Mr Cummings. She is far too contented where she is. She was the main instigator of our finding work here, the one who really wanted the job. I wonder if any of us will ever meet anyone we could possibly consider marrying?

12TH APRIL 1916 - TUESDAY

This evening I went to see May off at the station. Ida was there as well. No signs of Mr Cummings, thank goodness! When May went to supervise their luggage, a huge mountain of hat boxes and trunks, Vava ran about the platform in a panic, shrieking, 'Deakie, Deakie,' her pet name for May, thinking she had lost sight of her. Deakie, perhaps Miss Deakie if she is being polite, is May's name in the Sartisson household[2]. Everyone turned around expecting to see a pet dog. The Russians are very fond of diminutives so nearly everyone has a shortened form of their name, perhaps because the patronymic is such a mouthful.

Our surname is Dickinson which originates from Yorkshire but we are not such innocents abroad as people seem to think. My birth name, according to my birth certificate, was Marguerite Alexandrovna, really too much of a mouthful for our mother, who was born in Liverpool. It soon became Daisy in the family and Miss Daisy it remains. There are six in our family – five girls and a boy, all born in St Petersburg but we all left Russia in 1905 during the first outbreak of Revolution when our father lost all his money invested in the foundry where he was manager. According to my father the Dickinson family has been in Russia since 1800, probably before that when the first of my ancestors ran away from a farm somewhere in Yorkshire to join the Russian army. I often wonder whether he fought in the battles against Napoleon whose army marched on Moscow only to find that it was burnt to the ground.

After waving the train out as far as we could see, Ida returned home with me feeling sad because May had gone. Nina Michaelovna went out so we were able to have a confidential chat as Piotr Petrovitch was playing cards with some of his fellow officers and there was no chance he would be able to hear us giggling and gossiping. What a beautiful and useful object the samovar is. We sat drinking tea until quite late. Sometimes when they are both out, we try on Nina Michaelovna's beautiful hats in front of the long mirror in her bedroom, but tonight we had a lot to talk about.

2   Mrs Sartisson also had an English governess named Miss Deakon and this is probably where the name originated.

13TH APRIL 1916 – WEDNESDAY

Today I will describe as a day of incident. An officer named Arcardi Dmitritch Porowshin, whom I like very much, turned up back from the war on three days leave. He is a friend of the family. He is in the Imperial Horse Guards Regiment. After dinner we were in the sitting room when he arrived, smiling and so very young-looking. He asked if he could take me to the cinema and as Piotr Petrovitch was not at home, Nina Michaelovna agreed. It was such a lovely evening we went for a long walk instead. Most of my evenings are spent writing letters but tonight it is very late so I will try to sleep. Arcadi Dmitrich was brought up from a young age at the military school here in Petrograd and is where Petya will be going later this year.

14TH APRIL 1916 – THURSDAY

Again today has been a happy day for me, considering my daily routine. Adia, short for Arcardi, came to lunch. Nina Michaelovna decided I needed some fresh air after sitting with invalids for so long. I went for a walk by the river before visitors arrived in the evening and was left sitting with Petya and Natasha once again. At about 9.00pm, my sister Ida came and with her Adia, so we chatted in the sitting room whilst the others played cards. Ida entertained us with tales of the places she has worked at previously. Believe it or not, she had three places of work before the one she is in now. Her first place was with a Prince's family in the South, too far away from us in Petrograd, on a huge family estate. She was very lonely and soon fell ill with rheumatic fever. They kept her isolated in a summerhouse somewhere in the grounds until May received a telegram to bring her back here. She came to live with us at Nina Michaelovna's home until she was well enough to find another job. Ida is quite unlike our eldest sister May. She is such a dreamer and lot more delicate in health. She used to love dressing up in mother's hats and flirting with the boys and she hates writing letters. She was always the best one at giggling when we were supposed to be serious and our father would get very cross with her because she would make all of us start giggling.

At 11.00pm Ida got up to go, so Adia and I walked part of the way home with her and then drove back in a cab. It was another beautiful evening. Adia keeps on repeating, 'I do not want to go back to the war again.'

When we got home supper was being prepared. Adia always makes quite sure he sits next to me. Nina Michaelovna's four brothers and Piotr Petrovitch were all present when the latter started an argument about the war.

'And what are the English doing?' he asked, raising his eyebrows in my direction. He teases me continually about 'the English' and informs me all the time that Russia made an agreement or an alliance with France and England which guaranteed the western frontiers of Russia against German invasion.

I was so proud to see the British, French and the Russian flags flying together over Petrograd in 1914. The Russian army scored some victories when the Germans advanced on Flanders. Piotr Petrovitch is very fond of telling me that when the Germans tried to make a separate peace with Russia, the Tsar refused any negotiations and honoured his treaty with France and England. When Turkey entered the war on the German side, the Russian army held back the offensive of 134 divisions of the German army as well, without any help from their allies. Since then however, the Russian army is running out of ammunition, artillery and rifles. Piotr Petrovitch worries a great deal about this, I suppose.

Well, this being a military household they are all much better informed than I but I do read both the English newspapers sent by mother and the Russian ones too. They are always talking about the war here. I know that part of the Russian front is north of the Baltic against East Prussia, more than 550 miles long and it takes two weeks or more to transport the troops to the front. Anyway, I always stick up for England and answer him back.

The size of Russia, its actual geography, makes it impossible for the English to help and Russia has the biggest army in the world, millions in fact, I told him. He looks very surprised that I know anything about it. Well, I can't live here amongst all these brave uniforms and say nothing when Piotr Petrovitch growls at me in that sarcastic way he has. What are the English doing! Indeed! What Adia thought of me, I don't know. He just smiles at me.

15TH APRIL 1916 – FRIDAY

Today was the last day of Adia's stay. We went to church to pray for his safety, then with great reluctance he went off to say goodbye to his relatives. After dinner he rang up asking us to go to see him off so at 9.45pm we set off for the station. His last words were addressed to me. 'Write as often as you can, please Miss Daisy.' His mother was there shedding tears. No one knows his fate and he is so young. So many are being killed in the war, there is always the thought – 'What if he never comes back again.'

Most of my evenings I am glad to sit here in my room looking at the photographs of mother on my writing desk and wishing I could see her, wishing I could just float over into her house in England. I have a great many people to write to including two officers in the same regiment as Adia, the Imperial Russian Guard Regiment of the Chasseurs. One is Prince Gargarin, a visitor to our house, also an officer called Shoulkovski, as well as sending presents and gifts to some British sailors. There are so many counts and princes here in Petrograd, some from wealthy families, others impoverished playboys, most of them brought up at the Military Academy. Everyone writes and sends parcels to the front these days. My letters to mother are more frequent but we sisters receive ours from her in turn and pass them round. I do so love receiving letters as it breaks up the monotonous day but I am longing all the time to see mother again. I miss her so much. It is an impossible dream now even to think of visiting her and it is very strange to think that England is 14 days ahead of us here in Russia as we are still with the old style Julian calendar. In the rest of Europe and England the Gregorian calendar is in use so if we see a letter dated 1st April we always add on 14 days. Even so the post can take weeks – it is very slow.

Before the war started we were never able to save enough money. We each send one third of our wage every month to her. Then there are our dress-making bills, shoes, gloves, hats etc. Everything is so much more expensive these days. Long before we left England our father had become an alcoholic so one of the reasons we came here was to earn more money. I can't help wondering how they are coping in England and whether he has recovered or not.

17TH APRIL 1916 – SUNDAY

This morning we got up early and after church went for a walk. After lunch to the 'Children's World', a kind of playground, after dinner another walk, this time on the Nevski. Tomorrow we will be back to our old routine, lessons in the morning, dancing exercises with Natasha, walk out in the afternoon. The holiday is over thank God!

Mr and Mrs Loukin are out tonight, the servant is flirting with her boyfriend in the kitchen and I am left alone with the tick of the clock and Petia's snoring. I have no desire to sleep and just sit here thinking and take to scribbling in my diary.

I often dream about our childhood where we were born in the Vyborg district of Petrograd in a big wooden house on the banks of the Neva. The house adjoined the Phoenix Iron Foundry, a machine construction works where our father and his father before him were managers. They employed over 500 men. He was a man of great importance in those days, due to a big expansion of trade in machine production. It was the biggest industry in the city and its rate of growth was twice that of any other industry.

In the late 1880s our father travelled every year to Manchester where the Phoenix had a sister company. He was sent to inspect a huge cotton mill engine at the Sun Mill in Oldham, Lancashire, which was the biggest mill engine in the world. It was there, in that smoky, old cotton mill town that he met our mother who was working as a roller coverer at the Sun Mill. She always told us it was very strange how they met and discovered they had almost the same names. She was Frances Ann and he was Alexander Francis, both with the surname of Dickinson. The roller-coverer's job is sticking pieces of leather onto the rollers or reels which take the cotton. She was busy gluing pieces of leather when Alexander Francis caught her eye. She was so beautiful in those days with smiling dimples in both cheeks. She used to tell us stories about how she and her sisters had gone from Liverpool, where she was born, to work in the cotton mills of Oldham after her father died. There were a great many cotton mills in Oldham which all employed very young girls and women. Her stories often made us cry because they worked so hard and such long hours when she was a girl.

My mother arrived at the house on the quay, Numbers 39-41 Palustrovskaya Nabergenya (quay), in the late 1880s and it was there our family was born, five girls and one boy. We three girls, May, Ida and Daisy, were the first to arrive. 'My little Trio', she called us, born with about a year between each of us.

I know of no other country in the world where so many servants are employed. There was such a big intake of peasants from the country, all wanting to find work, we even had a boy to chop the wood for the stoves, one to polish the floors, one to set all the clocks and I even had a Russian wet nurse to feed me when I was born. After a few years mother grew used to a life of ease and luxury. She didn't need to lift a finger. I can never forget our nursemaid Annushka, who cried all day when we left there in 1905 to travel with mother back to Oldham where her sisters were still living. I was just thirteen years old when we left. It was the end of my childhood.

I remember how our father went out quite early one icy morning to find his assistant manager, Mr Pudan, lying face down in the snow with an axe in the back of his head, murdered by one of the revolutionary workers. Soon after that almost the whole of St Petersburg was on strike and marching in the streets. Father thought it was no longer safe for us to stay there.

The revolutionary workers at most of the engineering works had established themselves like trades unions with deputies in each factory. A man called Semonov was the deputy at the Phoenix and there was also the famous Father Gapon, a kind of militant priest, who went about organising meetings and urging the strikes. He also urged our father to become a Russian citizen but father never would. He hung onto his British passport, I suppose because of his work.

1904-5 was a kind of landmark in Russian history. On 9th January, a peaceful demonstration of workers carried a petition to Tsar Nicholas II, only to be met by bullets and what amounted to a massacre of innocent people which became known as Bloody Sunday. Everyone was outraged at this especially our father. A disastrous war with Japan had started in which half the Russian fleet was sunk. This was how our father spent his last years in St Petersburg, worrying about our safety and the fact that all his money was tied up in shares and insurance policies in the Phoenix.

12

Mother packed all her precious china and the porcelain figurines she had collected and wearing her long sealskin coat which almost touched the ground, she waved goodbye to father, as did all six of us.

We were boarded out with mother's sisters when we arrived in Oldham, a dismal, dirty, old town, full of cotton mills and tall chimneys belching out long ribbons of smoke everywhere. We had very little money and I found out later that our poor mother was existing on bowls of sago. We were entirely dependent on mother's sisters. Father wrote to say that it was impossible to retrieve his money and he had decided to go to Chile, South America, where they were giving away land and all he had to do was make a claim. His own father and brothers had already gone there, made claims and were doing well.

My father said that a man called Stolypin had become prime minister and the Tsar, the supreme autocratic ruler who makes all the government decisions, had made some kind of land concessions to the peasants. The revolutionaries were being rounded up and hanged or thrown into jail; 'Stolypin's neck-ties' is what the hangings were called. So the uprising of the workers slowly disintegrated. Things have not changed very much as far as I can see; there is still a lot of political unrest but the war is the main focus of attention for most people just now, at least in this house it is.

Well, it is almost 2.00am and so I shall try to sleep. I think I have developed insomnia over these last few months.

19TH APRIL 1916 - TUESDAY

I felt very tired today. Well I would after so much talking has gone on this Easter holiday and I have been wishing for this evening to come. After lunch I got a letter and a postcard from Adia. He dare not write much as he knows that Nina

Michaelovna reads all my letters but I have found a very good hiding place in my room for this diary and his letters. I wonder whether he will ever come back again.

20TH APRIL 1916 – WEDNESDAY

Sometimes I get up and feel as though the duties of the day are just too much. It may seem strange but I can think of nothing interesting to say. Nina Michaelovna and I have not been speaking to each other all day. We did not quarrel exactly but I happened to forget a phone call she asked me to make. When I did, of course the bird had flown and I was blamed for it. Anyway, I am not going to speak first. Maybe it's very stupid of me, but no I will not. Even so, I feel horrid about it all tonight. I said 'sorry' – what more does she expect of me. Sometimes I get so tired of life with the children.

23RD APRIL 1916 – SATURDAY

A day spent mostly outdoors, thank goodness! In the morning we were at the town hall for a rehearsal of Natasha's dancing. I have been very busy making the costumes ready for tomorrow and practising steps with her. The ballerina who teaches her was there and applauded loudly. We have been learning the national dances of various countries as well as the Russian one. I have not had any time to myself at all. Nina Michaelovna is still cross with me about the phone call.

24TH APRIL 1916 – SUNDAY

Natasha danced very nicely and had much applause. When we came home, we dined and then I put both children to bed.

Nina Michaelovna offered to stay at home, believe it or not, so that I could go out to meet Ida. At last all is forgiven. Ida was so glad to see me. She has such a lot to contend with at her place on Morskaya street where she lives in a huge apartment on the first floor of a very imposing building at number 59. This street is very well known in St Petersburg for the fact that both Gogol and Dostoevski lived there in the 1800s – not to mention Tchaikovsky, who composed his symphony 'Pathetique' on the top floor at number 13, shortly before he died in 1893. Nina Michaelovna told me about this. Ida works for the family of Pistolkors, a very well connected family, amongst the elite of Petrograd high society, where she has been living for the last four years. Alexandra Pistolkors is the mother of three adorable little girls – Sandra the eldest, is six, Olga is four and Tatiana, her mother's favourite, almost three years old. Alexandra or Aylia as she likes to be called, is the sister of the notorious Anna Verubova – notorious because of her close friendship with the Tsarina and she has lived for many years in a small house in Tsarskoe Selo (the Tsar's village) close to Alexander Palace, home of Tsar Nicholas and Tsarina Alexandra, where Ida takes the children to visit their aunt and where they play with the Tsarina's daughters.

Well, two such different sisters you could never imagine. Aylia is very beautiful, like a china doll most people say, whereas Anna is rather plump with double chins and a very thick set, square face. However they are both united with the Tsarina in their implicit trust and faith in Father Gregory – or Rasputin as he is referred to in the newspapers which report the most scandalous stories about him. Rasputin in Russian means 'rascal' or 'rogue' – so it's not really appropriate to call him by that name because he is a kind of travelling, holy monk capable of performing amazing miracles for those who believe. At least that is what Anna Verubova tells Ida. In 1915 Anna was badly injured in a train crash. Pulled unconscious from the wreckage she lay in a coma for several days with broken legs and back. The doctors said she could not possibly survive. The Tsarina summoned Rasputin to her bedside. He called her name three times and she opened her eyes. 'She will live but will always be a cripple,' he said. With the help of his prayers she began to recover. Since then she walks with the aid of a crutch or is taken about in a wheelchair. Her faith in Rasputin is unshakeable. She also likes to talk about her ancestors and make sure everyone knows she has quite a long, hereditary connection with the court. Their family name is Taneyev and her father is Director of the Imperial Chancellery, an office held by his father and his grandfather. Their mother is the daughter of General Tolstoy, aide-de-camp of Tsar Alexander II and one of their ancestors was Field Marshal Kutusov, a very famous hero of the Napoleonic Wars – not only all this but her father and uncle are also quite famous musicians, her uncle being the favourite pupil of Tchaikovsky and even more infamous, Ida says, for his affair with Tolstoy's wife. This love affair became the inspiration for Tolstoy's story, 'The Kreuzer Sonata', because one of the characters in it named 'Trookashevski' was believed to be based on Sergei Taneyev. Anna Verubova is 10 years younger than the Tsarina – 34 at her last birthday. Some years ago, about 1907, she was married to a young naval officer, Alexander Verubov. The marriage was approved and encouraged by the Tsarina but ended in divorce less than a few months later. According to the gossip in Tsarskoe Selo, the marriage was never consummated but she still uses the married name of Verubova.

The Tsarina's second daughter, Grand duchess Tatiana is godmother to Aylia's first daughter and all three are very much spoilt by their aunt, having many birthday and nameday (christening day) presents and parties. The Tsarina asks Ida a lot of questions about our family and her childhood because her own family of four girls and one boy is not unlike our family of five girls and one boy in which the two youngest Maria and

Anastasia seem to play together like our two younger sisters Vara and Ella.

Ida likes the Grand Duchess Maria best of all who says that Ida will be her children's governess when she marries and that she will send for her where ever she may be living – All the Grand Duchesses talk about who they are going to marry. Maria thinks she will probably marry Louis Mountbatten and will perhaps live in England. Ida says she is very fond of giggling and flirting with the Cossack guards but of course no one dares put a foot out of place when the Tsarina is there. And it seems very strange to me, no one ever mentions the fact that perhaps one of these lovely girls may be the carrier of that terrible disease haemophilia which their little brother Alexis suffers from. It is quite well known that this disease is carried through the female members of the family.

Anna Verubova's house in Tsarskoe Selo is always full of exotic flowers which are sent every day by the Tsarina, grown in the Royal conservatories. We do not see one blade of green here in town until Easter or often much later in the year.

We had a lot of things to talk about tonight and I am hardly in the mood for sleeping – There is such a web of intrigue and jealousy surrounding Anna Verubova, I am afraid for Ida's safety. Most of the intrigues centre around Anna Verubova's close friendship with the Tsarina and her relationship with Father Gregory. She tells Ida that he is truly a man of God who has been sent to them and it is only through his prayers that Alexis can be cured from his attacks of haemophilia which cause such great pain. When Father Gregory says prayers at his bedside, the little boy is seen to recover immediately, whilst all the best doctors in the land can do nothing to provide a cure.

The secret police watch Father Gregory and all his associates. Ida and I always talk in whispers about this mysterious religious group called 'the Khlist' which he is rumoured to be a member of. It is something quite sinister, we are sure of that. They believe it is only through sin one can gain redemption in the eyes of

God, so we both wonder what kind of sins they all manage to get up to, especially Aylia with all her secret love affairs. There are a great many aristocratic ladies visiting Father Gregory's house on Gorokhovaya Street. A lot of them go there just to find favour with the Tsarina. Some go with petitions begging favours for their husbands and children, hoping for higher positions – money changes hands. Father Gregory runs to Anna Verubova who tells all to the Tsarina and lo and behold their wishes are granted and another miracle has taken place. Since the Tsar is away at Army headquarters even members of the Duma (Russian parliament) seem to be chosen this way.

Anna Verubova sends a car to the Morskaya for Ida to take the children to Tsarksoe Selo, which is situated about 16 miles south of Petrograd and contains many beautiful palaces. The biggest and most imposing is the Catherine palace, once home to Catherine the Great. The smaller one, the Alexander palace where the Tsar, Tsarina and their family live is surrounded by very beautiful parks, gardens and lakes. Princess Paley and Grand Duke Paul, the Tsar's uncle, also have a palace there, not on such a grand scale as the Alexander palace but filled with antiques and paintings they collected during their exile in Paris. Princess Paley (as she became after her divorce from Eric von Pistolkors and her marriage to the Grand Duke), is the mother of Ida's employer, Alexander Pistolkors and grandmother to Ida's three little girls. This is the other place she visits quite often in Tsarksoe Selo. Nearby is another imposing dwelling which may be referred to as a palace, where the Grand Duke Vladimir (another uncle of the Tsar) and his wife live. There is also a small town with numerous villas and streets.

Sometimes the four daughters of the Tsarina are there in the gardens which since the war began are not as well kept as before. Most of the men and gardeners are being drafted into the army, but it is a very beautiful place in the summer. Rasputin, who visits frequently to see Anna Verubova, can often be seen wandering amongst the trees. It is a far cry from life in the city – a pleasant escape. He has a reputation for seducing nursemaids, so people are always teasing Ida and asking questions about it – not a pleasant situation – but she will not leave the Pistolkors family because of all the trouble she had in the first three positions she took when she first came here.

Everyone has gone to bed. The house is silent. It is 2.00am.

25TH APRIL 1916 – MONDAY

Today we have been to look at a villa in the country at Kuokkola which is by the sea in Finland. We will most probably be spending the summer there. I am not overjoyed at the thought. It is so lonely there and I don't care how long we stay in town. Most people have dachas or rent apartments in Finland during the summer months. As children we used to go to Terijoki every summer and though I have such fond memories of the place, it always seems far too long a time to be away from town.

A lot of people, especially in England, think we have such very good jobs and live in comfort here but it is far from the truth. Our lives are not our own any more and most of us grow old, turn into old maids or spinsters and even continue with the offspring of the children we once taught. Our friend Elizabeth Waters, came here when very young and she is now about 50 years old. She has just managed to save enough money to buy a small house on the outskirts of Petrograd. What a long time to be saving up her money! I don't think I could live like that. On the other hand, we have a good reputation here and are much in demand. The English governess is considered to be the very best, far better than the French or German. They secretly admire the English stiff upper lip, even if they do make fun of it, not to mention the impeccable manners we always teach and the fact that the Tsarina herself, who is the granddaughter of Queen Victoria, was brought up by an English governess. We are very proud of this and maybe some of us tend to overdo it a little bit, sometimes.

Today Shoulkovski rang up to say he is on three days' leave so perhaps he will bring me a letter from Adia.

26TH/27TH APRIL 1916 – TUESDAY/WEDNESDAY

The days spent as usual and wishing for this hour when the children are in bed. I wish I could be more contented like my sister May. This evening Shoulkovski arrived and with him Nina Michaelovna's brothers so we sat and talked most of the evening. They talked about the war and teased me a great deal about the English doing nothing again!

28TH APRIL 1916 – THURSDAY

Both my pupils are ill and it has been very dull staying indoors all day. I think they have influenza this time. 'Miss Daisy, Miss Daisy' they are calling out all the time.

29TH APRIL 1916 – FRIDAY

I have not felt very well all day. We stayed in the house all day. My head felt dizzy and now I am writing this in bed.

5TH MAY 1916 – THURSDAY

Spending my time in bed feeling dizzy and very lonely as I cannot even read, even this writing has tired me out. Maybe Ida will come to see me.

6TH MAY 1916 – FRIDAY

This morning I got up feeling a little better and was so glad to hear that Adia has arrived back and will be calling. He has some injury to his leg which happened because his horse was shot from under him.

12TH MAY 1916 – SATURDAY

Adia brought his brother who is also rather nice and we all went to the zoo with the children. He came home with us and had dinner, after which we went out walking on the Nevski. We live not far from the Bankovski Bridge. It has two huge, cast iron griffons at each end. We cross this to reach the Nevski Prospect. Adia is limping quite badly as his knee and ankle were injured – not broken but quite badly crushed and bruised – so one leg I swathed in bandages and he has a stick to help him walk. He will be here at home now for a few weeks probably whilst he recovers.

13TH MAY 1916 – FRIDAY

Went to see my other pupil Veronica today where I give extra lessons in English. Then I had an appointment at the dentist's and who should be waiting for me but Adia with Nina Michaelovna and Natasha. After lunch we went to Natasha's dancing class and in the evening he got tickets to go to a concert.

14TH MAY 1916 – SATURDAY

Not a day passes without Adia. At 4.00pm his mother came to visit with her two other sons and after dinner we all went off for a drive round the Islands. I have no time to do anything as Adia is here every day and turns up in the evening as well. We will soon be going to the country, to Kuokkola in Finland, that is. I shall be sorry and glad, I don't know which.

20TH MAY 1916 – FRIDAY

Nothing special happened during the last few days. Most of my time spent with Adia and the children. Today I went shopping for summer clothes. I am afraid I will have very little money left after I have paid all my dressmaking bills; everything is so expensive these days. Adia has not been on the scene today and somehow I have missed him. Apparently he has gone to see a doctor for a medical examination. Thank God it was the horse and not Adia – a very lucky escape for him. He will most likely have 2 or 3 months leave.

21ST MAY 1916 – TUESDAY

This is the first day I have not seen Adia. It rained all afternoon. Yesterday I bought a new hat and now all I need is a rose to go on it.

This evening my sister Ida arrived. We had tea in the dining room and a little time to talk alone. She gets quite upset at times because Aylia sees so little of the children. Her husband, Alexander Pistolkors, is away at the war most of the time and Aylia is left to her own devices which include numerous affairs. Ida asked me, 'What does nymphomaniac mean?' We had to look it up in the dictionary; I had never heard of it before. Ida had heard it mentioned by some visitors who called whilst Aylia was out. There is such a lot of gossip goes on amongst the servants there, she doesn't know what to believe.

As for the children's father, well, he has the most illustrious reputation as an army officer and is often talked about in our house. He is very well known for his bravery but is also well known as very fierce and cruel. They say he shot eighty-five Latvian rebels with his own hands! When the war began he enlisted in the famous 'Wild Division' under General Kornilov and has been to the furthest point reached by the Russian troops, so now he has done two years of battles in the most terrible conditions. Ida says he is always quite jovial when she sees him. I suppose he is glad to be back home to see his 3 little daughters.

His background is quite a topic of conversation in our house with Nina Michaelovna and is well known by most people in Petrograd. He is the son of Captain Eric von Pistolkors, an army captain and *aide de camp* to the Grand Duke Vladimir, the Tsar's uncle. His mother, Olga Valerianova, caused a huge scandal many years ago, when she began a love affair with another uncle of the Tsar, Grand Duke Paul. Captain Eric von Pistolkors was left with a choice of resigning his commission and leaving the army or divorcing his wife who was already pregnant with the Grand Duke's child. He chose the latter.

Alexander and his sister Marianne von Pistolkors were brought up in Tsarskoe Selo, he at the Military Academy, whilst Olga and Grand Duke Paul were banished from Russia by the Tsar. They had what is called a morganatic marriage without permission from the Tsar and Grand Duke Paul lost his position, his income and his right to live in Russia, until shortly before the war began in 1914 when they were allowed to return. They spent their years of exile in Paris. Olga was created Princess Paley and their son, Vladimir, who could not take the Romanov name is now known as Prince Paley. They built a huge house, that is a palace, in Tsarskoe Selo, which they filled with antiques and paintings collected in Paris where they had lived with their two younger daughters Natalie and Irene. The ballroom of this palace is now turned into a workroom where Olga presides over ladies making gifts and presents for the troops. Ida takes the three girls there to see their grandmother. The Grand Duke Paul was a widower at the time of their marriage, with two children, Marie and Dmitri, from his first marriage to Princess Alexandra of Greece who died in childbirth.

Because the name von Pistolkors sounded too German, they dropped the 'von' in much the same way that Petersburg became Petrograd when the war started. Somehow, you see, they are all related, either by blood or marriage, to the Tsar and to what ever goes on in Tsarskoe Selo.

I saw Ida part of the way home to that huge apartment on the second floor of the house on the Morskaya. It looks so forbidding at night. Mr Forrest, the head chauffeur, was just arriving with Aylia as we stood on the corner. There are two or three nursemaids on duty at night for the children. I didn't want to leave her and shed a few tears on the way back partly due to feeling homesick and wondering what will become of us.

22ND MAY 1916 – SUNDAY

This morning was spent with Adia and the children. Went to church and then a walk. At 12 noon we set off to visit Uncle Constantin where we had lunch and then walked home. In the evening Adia came to see us again. He asks such a lot of questions about why we left Russia in 1904. I told him the whole sorry story more or less truthfully – no reason to lie about it – how our father lost all his money at the Phoenix engineering works and then went off to Chile and became an alcoholic – how we had no money and why we decided to come back to St Petersburg to work as English governesses. Whether this will make a difference to the way he feels about me remains to be seen. He then wanted to go out to the islands but Natasha was too tired. The Kamenny and Yelagin islands are beautiful places to visit, a great escape from town, with botanical gardens and parks and even Peter the Great's huge oak tree, which he planted in 1718. I was disappointed not to be able to go. Now Adia has just gone so I will write some letters tonight.

25TH MAY 1916 – WEDNESDAY

I have been busy preparing our things to take to the country and putting all my clothes in order before we leave on the 27th. It seems Adia has an aunt living in Kuokkola and will visit us there. Today has been spent packing, rushing to post letters and a lot of confusion. The children are over-excited, Nina Michaelovna distracted and Piotr Petrovitch in a very bad temper. Adia seemed to be amused by it all and not in the least upset at our departure. He says he will see us very soon. I wonder when that will be. Piotr Petrovitch is so short tempered and does not like the haphazard way we pack everything. He has asked me at least half a dozen times if I remembered to pack the ink.

27TH MAY 1916 – FRIDAY

I got up very early this morning. It has been such a bustle all day. We arrived in Kuokkola at 3.00pm. On the following train came Nina Michaelovna and Adia. Our things had not arrived owing to the fact that the servant forgot her passport, so Nina Michaelovna had to go back to town to find out what had happened. Adia, the children and I were left to fend for ourselves.

After I had put the children to bed and since it was one of those brief moments when we were alone, he ended the evening by saying that he loved no one else but me and that he was planning to leave the Guards' Regiment. I tried to make him promise that he would do no such thing but he refused. He will leave the Guards he says and will marry me. Marriage! I haven't even thought of it. All he has done up to now is hold my hand occasionally so this was quite a sudden and unexpected declaration. I did not know what to say to him. In that case, he said he would return to the war and be killed or he would shoot himself. He was quite dramatic at this point and looked as though he really meant it. I was so tired after the day's events that all I could do was make him promise he would not leave the Guards' Regiment and tell him that I could not think of marriage. He has now gone off looking black as thunder to his aunt's house, only a short distance away where he will stay. He will come back again on Sunday or Monday. What on earth am I to do!

29TH MAY 1916 – SATURDAY

Today has been a very busy day spent unpacking everything. Piotr Petrovitch arrived and raised a whole big row about things in general. We have no ink, one of the things I forgot to bring, so I am scribbling away with a blunt pencil by the side of a very smelly, little oil lamp on the table. Miss Daisy, Miss Daisy, where is the ink? Piotr Petrovitch is furious because I forgot to pack it and delivered a long speech about making lists. My window is open and I can hear the train in the distance. It is so quiet and still. We are at the far end of Kuokkola and it is very lonely. The war and all the bustle of Petrograd seem far away. We have a piano. Nina Michaelovna is playing a sad song.

30TH MAY 1916 – SUNDAY

I am awaiting news from everyone, from Ida, mother, May, so anxious for letters. Today we went on the beach playing tennis then for a long walk, the result of which is that my face and arms are quite sunburnt. In the evening Adia arrived and we set off for a long walk but it started to rain and we had to turn back. All the way home he insisted he would leave the Guards. I do not like to be threatened and held responsible. He is only 20 years old. I wish he was a bit older and wiser.

31ST MAY 1916 – MONDAY

Adia arrived about 3.00pm, so we went to the beach and had a game of tennis with the children. Piotr Petrovitch has gone back to town, thank God! Nina Michaelovna says I should not be seen with Adia so much because his relations will see us. He said he did not care very much what his relations will say and went off with some black looks. Nina Michaelovna already suspects what is going on, though really there is nothing at all 'going on' as far as I'm concerned.

1ST JUNE 1916 – WEDNESDAY

Adia went to town early this morning so I had some peace, if you could call it that. This evening he rushed in with flowers, lilies of the valley, tied up with a red ribbon. It was such a funny ending to the day. Now he is making it very obvious to everyone.

2ND JUNE 1916 – THURSDAY

I was left alone with my thoughts the whole day. Nina Michaelovna went off to town. Played on the beach with the children until dinner time. In the evening Adia came and we talked and talked on the same subject for about 2 hours. I'm so afraid that he is going to make a great deal of trouble. Of course,

I like him very much and admire him. He is so straight and honest, so urgent, so full of life, but as for love and marriage, I can't think that is possible. He is too young, he may change his mind at the drop of a hat and what would I do then? He says liking is akin to loving. I wonder what May would have to say about it. Here I am in the middle of nowhere, worrying about the future, when all I really want to do is go back to see mother and family again. I never thought when I left them that six long years or even more would pass before I saw them again or will I ever see them again and no one knows when the war will end.

3RD JUNE 1916 – FRIDAY

Today he landed here at 3.00pm and stayed until 10.00pm. It turns out that he has reported sick and will not go back to the war for a while. He swears he will shoot himself if I do not agree to marry him and I know very well his religious beliefs mean that when he makes an oath on the bible, which he says he has done, he is bound to keep it. I don't doubt he means it and will keep his word.

I always thought it would be so wonderfully romantic if someone was truly in love with me. Now I know how May felt when she gave her refusal to Mr Cummings. I am so undecided about what to say to him.

4TH/5TH JUNE 1916 – SATURDAY/SUNDAY

Two days of rain have passed. Adia spent most of them with us. A small boy came to see me about English lessons so I now have another pupil. It has gone very cold and we have not been out very much. Tomorrow I am going to town to see Ida. A day off at last! I cannot move or go anywhere here without Adia. It is really too overpowering and sometimes I feel I cannot breathe – Adia, the children, Nina Michaelovna – all very demanding. Not to mention Piotr Petrovitch and his eagle eye watching every small detail of our existence.

6TH JUNE 1916 – MONDAY

Today passed very quickly. Met Ida and we raced about the shops, then visited the dressmaker, then went into a café where we sat drinking tea with lemon and jam, listening to gypsy music which was very nice. Ida just wanted to tell me how she saw Rasputin last week in Tsarskoe Selo. She was walking along one of the paths, having left the children with Anna Verubova, when she saw him approaching from the opposite direction. As he came nearer, he held out his arms to her. Luckily, there were some trees and bushes close by, so she quickly disappeared into these hiding there until he had passed by. It is quite true to say that he mumbles to himself all the time as he walks along. Anna Verubova says he is praying. Aylia is a constant visitor at his house.

I have seen him in the street, once or twice. He is not much to look at; quite a dark, wrinkled face, a black beard with hair falling on each side of his face and a very big long nose. He strides along in wide Russian trousers and black boots, very well aware of his own importance. The whole of Petrograd talks about him and most people think he is a spy for the Germans, in league with the Tsarina who is not very popular either because of her German relations. It is a well known fact that he is able to hypnotise anyone who comes close to him and it is very unnerving for Ida.

There are some very funny stories going around, passed on from one source to another which are not printed in the newspapers. Several ladies including Aylia, who call on Rasputin at Goroknovaya Street, have remarked on the old leather couch which is in Rasputin's study, a small room adjoining the dining room where he receives petitioners. The leather they say is completely worn away and bare in parts and the back is broken away leaning against it. After guiding one of the ladies towards it, she sat down followed by Rasputin, who leaned against the back and with a loud crash it fell off onto the floor. 'You should get a carpenter to fix it,' she told him. 'Oh, it's all the fault of that lady from Simbirsk. As soon as she spends the night here it will fall of again,' he replied.

'Miss Ida,' Aylia says to her, 'you really should go to visit Father Gregory. He will pray for you. After church on Sunday evening you may come with me to see him.' Ida said she had an appointment to meet me on Sunday evening – 'You may bring Miss Daisy with you' she replied, so now I am involved in this ghastly dilemma,

There is no doubt he has the power of healing the young prince, but most people know he is just an illiterate peasant who has a wife and five children living in the village of Pokrovskoe in Siberia. In my grandfather's time during the 1840s and 50s, I'm quite sure Rasputin would have been sent to a penal colony in Siberia with four thousand lashes added to his sentence. Crimes against the state received the most cruel punishments in those days – 4,000 lashes! A flogging with rods or poles which many of them did not survive. Grandfather said they took it in stages of three to four hundred strokes, inflicted in one portion, and if more than five hundred then death was almost certain. They had to wait until their backs were healed before taking the next beating. Dostoevski, one of the greatest Russian writers, suffered this awful sentence but somehow survived it.

Ida's routine is much simpler than mine as Aylia rarely emerges much before 11.00am. The doctor is always the first in attendance, then the hairdresser and manicurist and sometimes the masseuse. Sometimes half an hour at lunchtime and bedtime is often as much as she can manage with the children. There are also two nursemaids on hand.

Ida has another fervent admirer in Count Andrei Komorowski, a Polish exile, who lives on Millionaya Street, number 25. How this street acquired its name seems quite obvious. At number 26, Grand Duke Vladimir lived and a very wealthy place it is. The Count Andrei Komorowski plays the cello and is often at the musical evenings we are invited to attend. He has also proposed marriage to her but has to be content in calling himself 'her favourite brother'. In this way no one is offended and the friendship continues.

We sat with our tea talking for a long time not wishing to move. When I told her about Adia, she wasn't in the least surprised. She has such a lot of admirers she manages to keep at a distance because she is not in love with any of them. The latest is one of the Montashov brothers who live in the apartment above her place; two oil millionaires from Armenia. She says they are very ugly. They used to throw big parties where all the ladies had an exquisite piece of jewellery at their place setting on the table. Aylia calls her 'English cold fish'. She can't believe Ida has turned down the advances of this man. There is a wide difference between her employer and mine. She has always been just Aylia to Ida, or often 'Poor Aylia' because she is rather like a spoilt, self-centred child. My goodness! If Ida carried on like she does, she would have been thrown out on the street by Alexander Pistolkors or his mother and made to find another job. She is still pursued by a Count Yourasov who leaps out of the shadows at every turn, begging her to marry him. I must say he is very constant with his letters and flowers but his name puts her off more than anything else and causes a lot of giggling when we see him.

'Can you just see our father's face if I was to introduce him?' she says. She met him when she was in the South of Russia, so he has been around for a long time now. She has another friend called Evald who is more like a brother to her than anything else and tries to look after her but he recently joined one of the Guards' regiments and went off to the war.

Ida had no solution to my problems but says I must not think of marrying anyone whilst the war is on. She says there is talk of food rationing in Petrograd now as most of the supplies are going to the troops. On my return, Adia was waiting for me at the station and has just gone back to his aunt's house.

10TH JUNE 1916 – FRIDAY

Today we went with the children to the 'Lighthouse', a place where they do all kinds of gymnastics and dancing. Natasha dances very well. The Russian dance is one of the most energetic with a lot of high leaps, then down to the floor with arms folded and legs kicking outward – needs a lot of practice to do with without losing one's balance – and I am very tired – it has been a busy day. On 18th June I am going to dance in the theatre here. We do our dancing exercises every morning with the ballerina's son. I am also learning how to bake bread. It will be useful if the food shortage comes about. Every day we play tennis on the beach with Adia. I gave my first lesson today to the boy pupil, a funny little boy who does more talking than learning and is very amusing.

11TH JUNE 1916 – SATURDAY

Piotr Petrovitch arrived for his weekend stay. The usual programme: dance exercises, study, beach, walk. Now I have just put the children to bed, Adia has arrived and so I will have to go and talk with all of them for the rest of the evening.

12TH JUNE 1916 – SUNDAY

Piotr Petrovitch was at home so it was 'long faces' day. It is 9.00pm. Adia is still here. Perhaps we may go for a walk which will end in the same way: 'I love you and no one else.' Two nights of talking about the war; there is more cheerful news. It seems the Russian troops launched an offensive on the South Western front under General Brusilov. He used a new tactic of breaking through the enemy defences by attacking from several different directions at the same time. Adia and Piotr Petrovitch got very much excited about this. They call it the 'Brusilov Breakthrough' and it is going to be admired all over the world. A lot of Adia's friends have died in the war. There is quite a different atmosphere when Piotr Petrovitch is here.

13TH JUNE 1916 – MONDAY

This afternoon Adia came with his two cousins who are very nice young girls. We all went to the beach and in the evening he rolled up again just as I got out of the bath. He said he would tell Nina Michaelovna that I had appeared in a very indecent condition. I bathed in the sea for the first time today and it was ever so cold. Now I am sitting on the balcony. No one is at home. This page is very dirty with blots of ink but I am not to blame. Adia is – for closing the book before I had finished writing and I was swept away.

14TH JUNE 1916 – TUESDAY

It is getting nearer my time to dance at the theatre and I am feeling quite nervous. We went to the Lighthouse to practise, then a walk along the beach. The whole day and evening spent with Adia.

15TH JUNE 1916 – WEDNESDAY

Adia went off to town. He says he will have to go back to the war very soon. Today has been spent mainly at the children's Lighthouse then on the beach. Tonight I am sitting on the balcony. It is a very beautiful evening, so quiet and still. No doubt I am a very ungrateful girl to grumble about my situation.

16TH JUNE 1916 – THURSDAY

This morning we practised the dance with Natasha. I like dancing so much. Two letters from May in Yaroslavl arrived. She is quite contented and well, not in any hurry to return to Petrograd. She is hearing dreadful things about what is happening and wonders if it is true. It is very much like what happened in 1905 in St Petersburg, when we had Father Gapon and a lot of strikes in all the work places. I wonder where she heard this – perhaps from Mr Sartisson.

17TH JUNE 1916 – FRIDAY

All day spent with the children at the Lighthouse and this evening with Adia. Everyone is very excited about tomorrow's performance at the theatre.

18TH JUNE 1916 – SATURDAY

In the evening I went to dance at the theatre, a Russian dance in national costume complete with beaded headdress and coloured ribbons at the back. I danced so well I was applauded and had to repeat the dance twice. Adia was there with Nina Michaelovna and children, my sister Ida and her boyfriend Evald also sat in the front row. so I did a great deal of smiling at them. My dress suited me so well. They said I looked just like a little Russian girl. If I ever go back to England I shall dance the Russian dance for mother.

After the dances on the stage had finished, Adia and I stayed on for the ballroom dancing which was to take place but as he is still on sick leave with an injured leg he could not dance. When we came home everything was very quiet and we went to look at the sea. He was very sad and begging me to promise to be his wife but I could not.

19TH JUNE 1916 – SUNDAY

Today has been such a long drag as I felt so tired after yesterday. We all went to the Lighthouse. At 6.00pm we went to the station to see Adia off to town. Another visit to the doctor to say he is ill.

20TH JUNE 1916 – MONDAY

It has been very quiet without Adia as he always makes such a lot of noise. Sometimes I feel so useless. The whole summer will pass in the same way like this and I am not doing anything useful. Nina Michaelovna floats along the beach in her white summer dresses and beautiful hats. She plays the piano and sings songs from the opera in Russian of course, very beautiful songs. She goes to musical evenings, visits friends, smiles and laughs with the children and has great patience especially with Piotr Petrovitch. Now Adia is doing his best to leave the Guards Regiment and what will he do then I wonder – drift about here in Finland or find some kind of job in another country? Perhaps I should look for another job but what would I do? Dance on the stage? It would be far too risky and would never pay enough money for me to send some home to mother. I am in such a rotten mood tonight. I feel like quarrelling with everyone. Now I can go to bed and have a good weep about everything in general.

23RD/24TH JUNE 1916 – FRIDAY/SATURDAY

We had our usual routine for the last two days but I did not feel like writing. Adia is still away in town. We paid a visit to his aunt with Nina Michaelovna and the children. I felt very silly as they all did a lot of staring at me, guessing I suppose at the situation with Adia. I had a letter from him this morning to say he will be coming back on Saturday – today. It was a very hot day. Piotr Petrovitch arrived this evening and we heard nothing but grumbling all the time he was with us. Certainly he does not seem to like holidays very much at all and is quite ill at ease here in the country. He is more used to having batmen and adjutants answering his every whim I think.

26TH JUNE 1916 – SUNDAY

Today we all went to bathe including Uncle Constantin who also arrived last night and took photographs of us in our bathing costumes. I hope they don't turn out. Adia came to the beach but did not bathe because he is still an invalid and just now asleep on the sofa.

29TH JUNE 1916 – WEDNESDAY

It was Natasha's Name Day so we did no studying, only our dancing lesson. After supper the people in the apartment upstairs came in and we had ice cream. There are two boys living there who also came and it was so jolly to have a laugh and joke with them but was sorry afterwards as Adia was very angry and jealous. I cannot speak to anyone these days or he becomes very cross. He does not know I am going to the 'Tennis Ball' with one of the boys on Saturday, so he will be furious. He is ill and cannot go.

30TH JUNE 1916 – THURSDAY

Cannot say very much about today. I received a letter from Shoulkovski who begs me to persuade Adia not to leave the Regiment and to go back to the war but what if he is killed – I would feel very bad.

1ST JULY 1916 – FRIDAY

Passed in the usual way. I am going to dance at the Theatre again next weekend, this time a Japanese dance and am busy making the costume.

2ND JULY 1916 – SATURDAY

I went to the 'Tennis Ball' with the boy from upstairs and danced a great deal. It was 3.00am when we came home. Everyone was asleep. I am afraid I will be in very great trouble tomorrow.

3RD JULY 1916 – SUNDAY

A very bad day. Piotr Petrovitch announced that they are thinking of going to the south in the autumn to Tiflis and wants to know whether I will go with them because bad times are expected in Petrograd. It was so sudden that I couldn't think what to say to him. I cannot bear the thought of leaving my sisters. He is most insistent I must go with them as the children would be lost without me. It is so hot today my head is aching. In the afternoon we went to the station to see Piotr Petrovitch off back to town, then to visit Adia at his aunt's house where his mother has arrived. The atmosphere was very tense and they stared at me all the time but no chance of talking to Adia alone, thank goodness! Apparently his mother told Nina Michaelovna I was 'very nice'!

4TH JULY 1916 – MONDAY

Another tedious day of lessons and dance practice. I am in such a terrible state of wondering what to do. They have not told the children and when I think of parting with them my heart breaks, especially little Natasha who has been brought up with me since a baby. I could not think of leaving my sisters to go such a long way to Tiflis.

8TH JULY 1916 – FRIDAY

I have been practising the Japanese dance as tomorrow I will have to appear at the Theatre. Adia has gone to town but he will come back tomorrow to see me dance.

9TH JULY 1916 – SATURDAY

In the evening I went to the Theatre to do the Japanese dance. I was not nervous. Adia came with some friends and his brother.

He gave me a big bunch of flowers all tied up with white ribbon. I was praised very much for the way I danced and I am very glad that I can dance well or understand the dance as they say here. It is pleasant to think you can do one thing well. Certainly I will miss all the dancing and music if I leave the Loukin family.

Letter from Ida came – she is upset I have not written and very worried because Aylia and Anna Verubova are begging her to go and have supper at Rasputin's house – I am also invited to go. I think they are doing this to show Princess Paley, the children's grandmother, who hates Rasputin, how much power they have over the household. If Ida refuses to go, it will be very uncomfortable for her when she visits Tsarskoe Selo – as for me, though I don't like the thought of sitting drinking tea with that smelly creature, I would go just for Ida's sake. Alexander Pistolkors is now violently opposed to Rasputin: so it seems Aylia and her sister Anna Verubova are on one side with Rasputin whilst Alexander, his mother Princess Paley and Grand Duke Paul are on the other: hating everything Rasputin stands for including his influence on the Tsarina. Many people think he is a German spy. All this causes a great amount of tension in the household – and now Ida is being dragged into it.

Also news from May who expects to be back from Yaroslavl any day now.

I am very tired tonight, more from thinking about what to do than anything else.

10TH JULY 1916 – SUNDAY

A very dull day spent in the usual way – Adia was flirting with a girl of thirteen named Tania on the beach. She is very pretty and everyone falls in love with her. I shall be very glad if he does fall in love with her. It will save me a lot of trouble.

11TH JULY 1916 – MONDAY

Went to my lesson with the boy and again was praised very much for the way I danced on Saturday. Adia is with us all the time and when he is not, he sends his orderly with letters for me. This afternoon he showed me the photograph of me he has in his locket, where I am looking angry as a bear. He says he is going back to the war in a few days time and wants to make sure I will go back to town to see him off. We went to see a hydroplane which had stopped on the beach – and then to see a huge fire at one of the villas which was burnt to the ground. Wooden houses burn up very quickly and crowds gather to watch.

15TH JULY 1916 – FRIDAY

Today we expected visitors from town – we were very busy preparing ice cream and cakes – had no time at all to do anything. Adia asked me to go to the Theatre but could not go. Nina Michaelovna has the most beautiful voice. She sings various arias from Italian operas in Russian. She has been practising. She will sing for the visitors tomorrow. Sometimes I join in and we make a duet – I have heard it so many times. We sing from La Traviata with great gusto and the children love it. She has given me a real love of both music and dancing. I suppose she has been like a second mother to me throughout all these years – and must admit, a very wise one. I am very fond of her and will miss her very much when they go to Tiflis.

17TH JULY 1916 – SUNDAY

What an awful day! I think I have never had a worse day. For one thing, it has been raining most of the time. This morning

I was surprised when Adia walked in. He said, 'I have come to say goodbye.' I could see that he was very much upset. After he had gone, I had to show a pleasant face to everyone and the day seemed so long – have got so used to him now. Tomorrow or Wednesday he will go back to the war.

18TH JULY 1916 – MONDAY

I felt very sad. He made up his mind so quickly yesterday and said he would call today but has not. We have heard from Petrograd that he is going tomorrow night and Nina Michaelovna has arranged that I should go tomorrow to town when I shall see him for the last time – felt so upset. I went down to the sea for a walk by myself but was even more upset when I came back.

21ST JULY 1916 – THURSDAY

When I got to town, Adia met me and we had to go to the Officers' Stores where one of the officers said he was to go today, then another officer came and said no, he was to go tomorrow. With that settled, we spent the whole day together in town, hardly knowing what to say to each other. At 9.30pm he said goodbye. How sad he looked. I cried all the way back to Kuokkola. I must start writing a letter to him now. He said letters take a very long time to reach the front.

22ND JULY 1916 – FRIDAY

Today was such an awful, dreary, long day. I did not want to wake up to it but had to go to my lesson and make a pleasant face. All I can do is pray to God that he will be safe. Added to this, we had to go to visit his aunt who asked me such a lot of questions. I think I might be called a good actress today. I am going to spend this evening writing to him as he will still be on his way to the war and thinking about those he has left behind. Somehow cannot think or write of anything else and must have turned into the most terrible bore these last few weeks. I feel as though something has vanished from my life and everything else is just a mockery. He gave me his gold christening cross, on which is inscribed, 'Save and Guard' in Russian.

23RD JULY 1916 – SATURDAY

Another dull, most monotonous day. This afternoon more visitors arrived and we had a great bother as the servant has disappeared back to town. I am about to spend this evening writing letters – can't even begin to think about what I am going to do when the family goes away to Tiflis. Maybe I could become a nurse in one of the Tsarina's hospitals for the wounded soldiers in Tsarskoe Selo.

24TH JULY 1916 SUNDAY

Today was the children's holiday show at the gymnasium. Natasha danced three dances. She was much petted and admired because she dances so well. I saw Adia's relations there and one of them remarked that I wasn't looking at all well. I received postcards from him today, still on the long journey to the front.

25TH JULY 1916 – MONDAY

Spent in much the same way. I am now learning a Spanish dance with the ballerina's son. When I see mother again, I will dance it for her. I wonder if I will be able to dance as well as last time.

29TH JULY 1916 – FRIDAY

Goodness gracious! How old I feel! Just imagine! I am 23 years old today. Could you ever believe it? Nina Michaelovna went off to town this morning and I wrote a letter to Adia. I cannot write properly when she keeps looking on. I have to race to the post. I received some nice little presents from the children and both tell me how much they love me. No letters from mother and father.

30TH JULY 1916 – SATURDAY

This morning we were up very early as we had to go to the shops for provisions because we are still without a servant. After that I gave Petya his English lesson and later visitors arrived from Petrograd. We sat a very long time at the dinner table and finished the evening playing tennis. I was expecting a letter but none came. Life goes on in exactly the same way with everyone.

When this holiday ends the only thing I can do is go to the Princess Alice Home in Petrograd which is the place where they allocate governess work. Ida has been there a few times. When we first started work here our positions were found for us by our great aunt who was still living in St Petersburg. As children, we had no grandmother so Great Aunt Adelaide, our father's aunt, became the matriarch of the family, the chief settler of disputes and source of all the things young ladies should know. She had been educated at the Smolni Institute where only the daughters of aristocratic families were allowed. She gained entrance to this imposing place because her father, our one great, illustrious ancestor, had fought in the Russian army and received many decorations for valour. He was presented with an ornate ceremonial sword by the Tsar Alexander II. He was given palatial living quarters in Kronstadt and married one of the daughters of a German banking family, who was a Baroness. Father often talked about him and the sword as one of his childhood heroes. I remember the ornate sword very well because it hung on the wall in one of the rooms of our house on Palustrovskaya Quay. Since Great Aunt Adelaide was the daughter of an army officer and a baroness to boot, she was well qualified to enter the Smolni Institute. She died in 1912 soon after I arrived here and I can still recall attending the funeral with her son Uncle George and his family. She was placed in a room where two more people were lying dead. We all had to hold a candle. When the priest started to sing and wave the incense about, I fainted and had to be carried out.

It was May who wrote to our great aunt asking her to find governess positions for us. Her good connections at the Smolni gave us excellent references and when the reply came, 'I'll see what my ladies can do,' May was all set to go. That was in 1909, I followed in 1910 and Ida in 1911. We could earn much higher wages in St Petersburg. Our father's drinking had been much worse since he returned from Chile where he went with our younger brother Leslie to make a claim on the land they were giving away. He had been unable to regain any of his money from the Phoenix. According to Leslie they arrived in a town called Lautaro where his brother had settled, to find it was little more than a row of shanty town buildings in the middle of a wilderness with a saloon, a general store and very little else. Whilst waiting for the claim to come through he began to drink more heavily and to realise that this was no place to bring up his teenage daughters; the claim did not come through in time and the money ran out so he had no other option but to return to Oldham where our mother was trying to survive with five daughters. She, of course, was overjoyed to see our little brother Leslie again, her only son and favourite child. When we went to live in the Corporation Arms, a small public house in Oldham where our father became landlord, she refused to set foot in the downstairs bars. By this time he had seen his dreams of a new life in Chile disappear and it was not very long before he found himself in the first stages of delirium tremens – seeing elephants on the ceiling and shouting 'Time gentlemen please' at 7 o'clock in the evening when we had to carry him upstairs to bed.

St Petersburg was much the same when we returned, an overcrowded, cosmopolitan city but looking back I suppose it is where we spent our happiest days of childhood.

I had a long walk by myself on the beach this evening. The moon was out and it all looked so beautifully calm and still. Homesickness is a real illness I think, curable by only one thing.

6TH AUGUST 1916 – SATURDAY

Nothing very much happened during the past week and have not much interest in anything – reading, tennis, dancing lessons. I have written two or three letters to Adia. I am making an Indian costume out of different coloured rags of material and feathers for the headdress for my next dancing performance. Tonight I went to a fancy dress dance. It was very nice but I know so few people. I went in my Japanese costume with my hair done up in proper style but did not dance very much.

7TH AUGUST 1916 – SUNDAY

Nothing much to say about today. Although it is the Sabbath, a day we should dedicate to God, am always glad when it comes to an end. I hate holidays in general but Sunday passes so slowly. We went to say goodbye to Adia's relations but do not like going as they always stare at me so much.

8TH AUGUST 1916 – MONDAY

Today had a letter from Adia in which he says I must write to my mother and father to tell them I am about to be married. Wish I knew what to do. I do not want to go south to Tiflis with Nina Michaelovna leaving my sisters in Petrograd. As for being married, which Adia now seems to take for granted, I can't even think of it and to receive letters like this from him do not know what to do. I feel so unsettled about everything.

9TH AUGUST 1916 – TUESDAY

This morning had another letter from Adia on the same subject – marriage. Nina Michaelovna is going to town accompanied by the children. I went to the station and saw them off and now am alone in the house. I can hear the sea – it is pitch dark outside and not a sound anywhere. I don't think I should like to live alone here with no one to speak to. My dance at the theatre is only 3 days away now. I have asked both May and Ida to come. Meanwhile must spend the next few days packing our things.

12TH AUGUST 1916 – FRIDAY

A day of days – Two letters from Adia – He has been to see the Commander to ask permission to marry! I am so afraid it will all turn out to be very serious.

Prince Gargagin arrived here with a wounded arm. He is going to stay a few days to recuperate but will come to see me dance tomorrow.

13TH AUGUST 1916 – SATURDAY

Very much excitement. May and Ida arrived at the Theatre – Dear May, whom I have not seen for such a long time. I did three dances but was applauded most for the Spanish dance which received an encore. I stayed on afterwards for the ball dances but know so few people there did not dance very much. Nina Michaelovna and the children came back from town to see me dance. Ida tells me I must set aside a date for supper with Rasputin when we get back to town. She has told both Aylia and her sister Anna that she will go to see him if I accompany her on some Sunday evening after church. Ida does not take this very seriously at all. She says we must be careful not to giggle! I don't think I will feel very much like giggling when the time comes.

14TH AUGUST 1916 – SUNDAY

A very weary day. Had a quarrel with Piotr Petrovitch who says I have not done nearly enough packing. We are leaving on Tuesday to go back to town.

16TH AUGUST 1916 – TUESDAY

Arrived back in town. It was raining and I was wet through. Our luggage has not arrived. I feel very much unsettled about changing my place and giving them a definite answer which I have not done yet. Ida's experiences when she first started work as a governess make me wonder whether or not I should apply for another post. She once worked for the family of Souvorin, editor of the *Novoe Vremia*, the most influential newspaper of the day, famous for the fact that it was the first one to publish Chekhov. Her employer was the son of the original editor and Ida called him 'the man with the golden smile' because he had all his teeth capped with gold. She was quite afraid of him. He kept snakes in the house as pets. She said they would suddenly slide out from behind a chair across the parquet floors and she had to try to stop herself screaming out loud.

There was one daughter who was very spoilt and pampered, continually running to her mother complaining that her hair had been pulled or some other kind of made-up stories. Ida would be very sharply reprimanded and became very upset about it.

Madame Souvorin was the talk of St Petersburg because she was the first woman to ride a motor cycle down the Nevski Prospect. She was absolutely mad on cars and would go roaring about the streets just for the fun of it.

The family was very much what is now described as Bohemian. Wild parties were held with a great deal of drinking amongst aspiring journalists, writers and poets. One moment the kitchens would be overflowing with expensive food and the next the cupboards would be bare. Sometimes, Ida said, there would not be a scrap of food left in the house. Mrs Souvorin would often be out and all the servants would either be asleep or entertaining their boyfriends in the kitchen.

After several months of this, Ida ran away and turned up on our doorstep. Nina Michaelovna took her in and she stayed with us for a few weeks before she found another post. I had to go to the Souvorin's and collect her things which was not a very pleasant journey to make. I remember standing in the room there, just hoping the snakes would not make an appearance because I would have screamed very loudly. Mr Souvorin flashed a glittering smile as I left.

17TH AUGUST 1916 – WEDNESDAY

Our things have still not arrived and we are all upset. Piotr Petrovitch is like an angry bear. We went to see Petya at his school where he is now a boarder. I wonder how he will like being away from home. I want to speak seriously to Nina Michaelovna but cannot pluck up the courage. She is so busy bustling about visiting people now we are back here. One thing I did manage to do was write a very serious letter to Adia asking how we are going to live without money 'if we do intend to marry' and saying that it would be better to wait until after the war is over.

20TH AUGUST 1916 – SATURDAY

Natasha has a cold so we have been at home all day. Another letter from Adia. He seems to take it for granted that we will marry and says it will be in December. He is now trying to change his regiment as quickly as possible, so he will be able to come home to see me. I have not decided about going to Tiflis and feel quite troubled about it. I have become so attached to this family and she is begging me to go with them. If I went, maybe it would solve the problem with Adia and things are getting much worse here as regards food shortages. Petia will stay at military school here.

24TH AUGUST 1916 – WEDNESDAY

I had four letters from Adia. They were brought from the country and older than the ones I have received in town. It is four days since I received a letter from him so something has gone wrong. We have not been out as Natasha has a bad cold –

most of the time spent reading. It is much quieter in the house now that Petya is away at school and we all miss him very much.

25TH AUGUST 1916 – THURSDAY

May and Ida have both written to say they do not want me to go to Tiflis – also a letter from Adia to say he is in the trenches and in battles every day so he has no time to write. He says it is beyond description there, a hell on earth.

26TH AUGUST 1916 – FRIDAY

This morning made up my mind not to go to the south. My little Natasha cried all day which has upset the whole house. It will be strange to go to another place after working here for so long. My nerves are on edge after all the crying. I am reading more books lately as it takes my mind off things a little.

27TH AUGUST 1916 – SATURDAY

Spent today reading in English. I had four cards from Adia in which he says he is still in the trenches, still in action and has little time for writing. This has been Natasha's Names Day. She had many presents. We went for a walk after a long session of reading aloud in English. I am now alone in my room. There are some officers playing cards in the sitting room and in the dining room a lady is sitting drinking tea with Nina Michaelovna. This morning I received two letters from HMS *Princess Royal*, from sailors who received some of the presents I made. One of them sent his photograph. I am glad. It will be a remembrance of this Great War. I made a lot of tobacco pouches out of leather for them.

30TH AUGUST 1916 – TUESDAY

Today I went to the Princess Alice Home to enquire about another place. This evening received a telegram to say that Adia is wounded and on his way home. No other details. It will be several days before he is brought back here and just pray to God that he is not too badly injured.

31ST AUGUST 1916 – WEDNESDAY

I went to see about a place today but was not very charmed with them. They talked too much. So when the lady rings up, I will refuse to go and have decided to go and stay with May at the Sartisson's in Terijoki for a week or two until I can find a suitable place.

We have been to the hospital where some of the officers in Adia's regiment are lying wounded but none of them knew anything about him, except to say that he is probably on the way. He must have been delayed on the way back. Once again must start packing my things; I have already packed my lovely, white, summer dresses and hats which are almost a trade mark of the English governess, also the smart gabardine coat which mother and father sent me for my 21st birthday. I have taken great care of it since I know it must have been so difficult and costly for them and it will wear for a few years yet. I have so much to do – Natasha is clinging to me all the time and I have no enthusiasm for packing. 'Miss Daisy, Miss Daisy, please come with us'. They are still undecided about the dangers of leaving Petia at the military school – where he enrolls in September. Piotr Petrovitch will stay here at the Admiralty.

4TH SEPTEMBER 1916 – SUNDAY

Adia rang up today. He is in the hospital. It seems he is not wounded but fell from his horse and injured his legs. He wanted me to go to see him today but it is impossible. This is my last day here. They leave for Tiflis tomorrow morning. I feel so nervous my hands are shaking. It is not pleasant to see the children cry and poor Natasha has been doing so nearly all day again. I will go to the hospital tomorrow but am so afraid to go alone and meet with his mother there. What on earth will she say to me about being married to her son?

5TH SEPTEMBER 1916 – MONDAY

It is now midday and have just returned from the station; cried the whole way back. Piotr Petrovitch is still here and gone to sleep. Now I have all my things to put away before tomorrow when I go to Finland to stay with May in Terijoki.

I have been to see Adia and found him quite thin and wasted, looking very ill. He was so glad to see me. His mother was not there and he is too ill to speak of any thoughts of marriage. I stayed for a while holding his hand. Most of his friends are dead, he says.

Feel so lonely. There is a dead silence in the house. I keep looking at all the boxes and that is as far as I go with the packing. Still have to ring the Princess Alice Home and ask them to let me know about a place when available and give them my new address. Adia considers that he is lucky to be alive. Most of his friends have died.

Everywhere looks so very drab in town after being in the country and on the tramcar coming back a fight broke out between some people arguing about food. They say the merchants are hiding some of the provisions and then putting the prices up when they reappear. People all over Petrograd are outraged by the appointment to the Duma of ministers who are selected, so they say, by Rasputin's influence on the Tsarina and are hated by almost everyone. The Tsar, who has absolute power over all decisions, is away at the Army Headquarters in Mogilev. Rasputin only selects ministers who are friends of his or who show loyalty to the Tsarina. A fine state of affairs when thousands are being killed in the war. Ida says the Tsarina looks very tired and worn and suffers from very bad headaches. The days when she reputedly spent most of her time lying on a chaise longue in her mauve boudoir are long gone. She and her daughters work tirelessly as nurses in the hospital during most mornings, also Anna Verubova, though both are in wheelchairs when out in the park in Tsarskoe Selo. She has never been very popular in Russia. Do not feel like sleeping tonight.

7TH SEPTEMBER 1916 – WEDNESDAY

Terijoki, Finland

Nothing very much has changed on the Podmener Estate since I visited here last year. It is very far removed from anything that is going on in the world. It is the most beautiful villa surrounded by trees and garden. Mrs Sartisson has been kindness itself saying I must stay here with May for as long as I want. She has just retired to her room with a fit of nerves as news has just come through that they are about to enlist men up to the age of 43 any time now. That would include Mr Sartisson who has so far been exempt. Like most of the ladies who employ a governess and tutors for their children, she is a superb pianist and is already asking me to dance at a family gathering she plans to hold one evening.

It is amazing how many tutors call here for Vava's education – French, German, mathematics, not to mention music and dance. Her education, like her mother's, is not for the purpose of finding work of any sort, as far as I can see, but mainly to impress a suitable husband with an appropriate family background. Physical attributes are of tremendous importance. You wouldn't believe how proud she is of Vava's profile which is called a Roman profile with nose and forehead in a perfect line. There is no doubt she is a very beautiful child having ash-blond hair falling in gentle waves to her shoulders, the most perfect features and big, violet-coloured eyes. They never step outside without hat, gloves and correct attire for whatever occasion. Hair brushing, at least a hundred strokes, takes half the morning. The placing of feet, knees and elbows is absolutely crucial and Vava is quickly reprimanded should she forget. May has grown used to this way of life. No wonder we are regarded as prim but it was not so much emphasised at the Loukin house, neither with Ida's family. This family is much more European than Russian.

Must write a letter to Adia. I cannot forget the awful scenes at the hospital where so many are dying from the most terrible wounds.

Feel so utterly useless in this boring, monotonous job. I wonder now whether I should apply for another but it all comes back to the question of money.

8TH SEPTEMBER 1916 – TUESDAY

I am beginning to feel a little calmer. It is very nice to be with May in this beautiful house and surroundings. She has the most beautiful room opening onto a balcony overlooking the garden.

10TH SEPTEMBER 1916– WEDNESDAY

No letters from anyone as yet but I suppose they will send them on from Petrograd. Been out walking with the dogs. Mrs

Sartisson arranged a picnic which reminded me very much of last summer when Ida and I visited here. A famous writer was here, Negley Farson who was in love with Vara, Mrs Sartisson's sister. She did not approve of him at all but he said he would write about the three governesses dressed in white in a book he was writing called '*The Way of the Transgressor*'. The love affair with Vara will not last long, I think. I am reading *A Tale of Two Cities*, which they say is the favourite book of the Tsar though I can't understand why.

Sat up until very late talking with May about the family and remembering our childhood in the big house next to the Phoenix Iron Foundry. We remember very little about our grandparents but May has some recollections of that time – we also talked about Rasputin.

May says that we should refuse to go for supper with Rasputin – she says that Ida does not realise that Aylia and her sister Anna are trying to influence the children.

We crept into our beds very late after everyone else was fast asleep.

16TH OCTOBER 1916– SUNDAY

Over a month has passed since I last opened my diary and so many changes have taken place since then. I came here on the 25th September and have now been in my new post for nearly two weeks. I am now in the Naval Cadet College which is a huge building near the Lieutenant Schmidt Bridge on Vasilevski Island, the largest island in the Neva delta. Our rooms on the first floor overlook the river Neva. I am working for the daughter of the Naval Minister, Ivan Constantin Grigorovitch, who has two children, Natalia (Toulia) and Andrei. Her husband is the director or head of the Naval Academy which houses over 700 student cadets. The family name is Kartzev. Mrs Kartzev's younger sister, also named Natalia, lives with them, so I have Big Toulia and Little Toulia to deal with.

I must thank God for placing me in such comfortable quarters although this place is so huge that it has taken several days to find my way around. It is much cosier in a smaller house. I am able to see Ida quite often as she is about 20 minutes walk away, over the bridge and am able to use the phone so can converse with May quite often. I have a lot more time to myself here as there is hardly any studying at all.

We are taken in a private car over to the Admiralty, one of the finest buildings in Petrograd, to see the minister Ivan Constantin Grigorovitch, a tall, very distinguished old man much respected and well thought of by most of the population, who almost worships his grandchildren and we visit at least two or three times a week. The minister's wife died when his second daughter, big Toulia, was nine years old – she is now aged 12. Mr and Mrs Kartzev go to dine there very often. I have a desk with a key where I can hide my diary.

17TH OCTOBER 1916 – MONDAY

Today, after taking the children to the Admiralty to see their grandfather – a weekly trip over the bridge – I called at Nina Michaelovna's to collect some of my things. It was very strange not to see Nina Michaelovna and Natasha and even more surprising to find just Piotr Petrovitch sitting there with Adia talking about the war! Adia made me rush off at once to have lunch with him at the Astoria. He will be returning to the war on 22nd of this month. He does not want to go as he is convinced that he will die. He has been three times to the front and twice come back injured. 'Who will you marry if I die?' he asks me.

19TH OCTOBER 1916 - WEDNESDAY

The children are getting quite used to me now. Sometimes they are a little capricious but must have patience. I received a letter from Natasha to say she misses me very much. I had a talk with Mrs Kartzev and told her all my problems, a tale of woe I suppose. She did not know what to advise me. They are more interested in Ida's situation and ask a lot of questions about her, saying that she is in a very dangerous position, surrounded on one side by the Pistolkors relations and on the other by Aylia, Anna Verubova and Rasputin. She says that on no account am I to go with Ida to visit Rasputin as he is constantly watched by secret police. Mr Kartzev said, very dryly, looking me up and down most critically, 'If you go, make sure you have a long spoon' – Rasputin is also known as the 'Holy Devil' in some quarters. Now feel very nervous about the whole situation and particularly for Ida. I would have to go secretly, since Mrs Kartzev is so much against it.

21ST OCTOBER 1916 - FRIDAY

I fully expected Adia to ring but he did not. Suppose I shall not see him to say goodbye because I cannot get away tomorrow. Perhaps it is better so because it is very upsetting to be at the station and see them going to the war.

22ND OCTOBER 1916 - SATURDAY

Surprised at no telephone call and felt very cross all day. No doubt I have been spoilt with attentions from him. Well, this afternoon a letter came. It seems he rang last night and no one told me so he has gone today on the 6.20pm and asks me to write often. I had an appointment to see Ida at her place which is a huge apartment furnished in the most magnificent style with the most beautiful icons and paintings. Some other people were present and Aylia told our fortunes, reading our palms very intently but it was the usual forecast – we would marry very tall, dark, handsome men, sail across seas and have three or four beautiful children. She is such a frivolous, silly little thing, with her hair always immaculately set in waves and curls. She is amazed that Ida has turned down the advances of one of the Montashov brothers who has made several proposals of marriage.

One of the guests was Maria Golovina whom Aylia introduced as Munia. She is related to the Pistolkors family and noted as one of Father Gregory's most devoted followers. Aylia made a special effort to tell her fortune because everyone knows she is such an unfortunate lady in regard to her love affair with Felix Yousopov's brother Nicholai. Nicholai was killed in a duel, believe it or not, many years ago but she can still never forget him. Father Gregory prays with her. She was going to enter a convent but he persuaded her not to do this because she has such a busy social life and wears the most beautiful dresses and hats, of which she has many. Such a very romantic story. Poor Munya! She was also told she would meet a tall, dark and handsome man but she shook her head from side to side when Aylia said this. Father Gregory calls at the Pistolkors' apartment quite often to see Aylia whilst her husband is away at the war. Ida keeps the children well out of the way in the nursery and makes excuses if she is called out. She says that he is a very frightening spectacle to see especially for the children, in spite of his religious crosses and over-familiar greetings to everyone because he has black, greasy hair which falls to his shoulders and a very unkempt beard and moustache through which he mutters some kind of prayers on behalf of whoever takes his hand. It is decided we will go for supper with Rasputin – Father

Gregory I must remember to say – on the Sunday after next, immediately after attending the church service, when we will receive a blessing from him to keep us safe in the hard times to come.

Aylia's husband is returning from the war very soon now as the doctors say he is suffering from battle fatigue and will need to rest. I wonder what she will do then and whether her sister has any idea of how many affairs she carries on. I am quite sure Anna Verubova would disapprove because she is so religious in her beliefs. I was glad to get away in the end. I do not know how Ida puts up with Aylia. I am sure I would be very tempted to give her a piece of my mind.

23RD OCTOBER 1916 – SUNDAY

We go to church in the college. It is a very moving sight to see so many of the young cadets praying. I spent the day quietly – went to see Petya – he looks much taller and more grown up and says he likes the school he is in very much. He looks so smart in his uniform and couldn't help a few tears falling when I left.

24TH OCTOBER 1916 – MONDAY

I am growing more accustomed to my situation as I have many more comforts. Today May was in town so we went for a glass of tea and a chat. She is invited to the wedding of a friend and I am also asked to go with her. May will be a bridesmaid. She is quite excited about it as it will take place next Saturday.

No letters from Adia. I expect he will be writing to me soon.

I am reading a very interesting book in English called *Sir Godfrey's Granddaughter*.

A very jolly day. We had a great deal of fun. The bride looked very pretty and the wedding ceremony impressed me very much. I did a lot of singing and dancing. May looked wonderful in her bridesmaid's dress and I couldn't help wishing it had been her wedding. Mr Cummings was there and she is invited to his house. Perhaps he thinks she will change her mind.

There was a letter from Adia when I came back. I thought he could not have forgotten me so soon.

Today the Town Hall opened. As we were expecting trouble in the streets we did not go out with the children. Large crowds are beginning to gather making protest marches. There are a lot of very angry people out there. I am not afraid to go out but cannot risk taking the children. Some people are very much against the Tsar who once was thought of almost like a God – some are against the government and some are shouting out against Rasputin. The food shortages are making things very difficult. I don't know how the poor people manage to pay such high prices for things. A phone call from Ida. Our appointment with Father Gregory is postponed. It seems Pistolkors arrived back home from the war last night and there was a huge row which could be heard all over the apartment. It ended with Aylia flouncing out and being driven to her sister's place in Tsarskoe Selo. Soon after this, the children's grandmother, Princess Paley arrived to see her son and a long conversation took place about Aylia and her sister and their involvement with Father Gregory. They are afraid of the influence he may have over Ida and the children. Aylia is very determined to have her own way or should I say used to having her own way. Of course she does not wish to upset the Tsarina. Alexander Pistolkors has been away at the war for so long. 'Poor Aylia!' The Tsarina has either friends or enemies there is no inbetween – everything is quite black or white and Father Gregory is 'our friend'. I don't know what will happen now but Ida is caught in the crossfire.

At last a letter from England arrived. Leslie, my little brother, is in the Fleet Air Arm and is being sent abroad. Mother will be so upset. She says father has stopped drinking – is much better and looking for a job – some good news at least. I am never in bed before 1.30am here. It is a habit now that somehow I am unable to break; make a resolution every day to go to bed earlier but always break it.

4TH NOVEMBER 1916 – FRIDAY

I have just been looking at the orange blossom from the wedding in a glass on my table next to my mother's photograph and so many memories seem to crowd into my head. Every week now we visit one of the hospitals taking presents of food for the wounded soldiers. One of them had been there for four months, with leg injuries. No news from Adia. I wonder where the orange blossom comes from? Somewhere far away.

8TH NOVEMBER 1916 – TUESDAY

We have been indoors all day. There is a keen frost. Nothing special happened. It is very dull to sit in the house all day long. The children have been playing a game of Lotto and have just been put to bed. I shall spend the evening writing letters.

14TH NOVEMBER 1916 – MONDAY

The children have been ill. We have not been out. The days have been dull and monotonous. Time drags very much. I spoke to May by phone for a long time today and wish I could be contented like she is. Adia must be in a very bad mood not to write to me so often.

We see very little of Mr Kartzev because he is working in his office most of the time.

15TH NOVEMBER 1916 – TUESDAY

Today received two letters from Adia. He is in the trenches and says that getting my letters is the only pleasure he has.

Have been thinking how lonely our life is, going on for six years we have not seen mother and father. The war is so awful – the streets are darker and in nearly every street are queues of people waiting for meat, butter, sugar or bread. I don't think it is like this in England – Not been out as children are ill.

19TH NOVEMBER 1916 – SATURDAY

Went to dinner at the Sartissons' apartment. There were a lot of visitors and I danced the Russian dance three times for them with much applause. Ida was there and it was quite a jolly sort of evening.

22ND NOVEMBER 1916 – TUESDAY

I met Ida today and we had tea in a café and a good talk about things in general. Uncle George, Aunt Adelaide's son, phoned to say he and family are back in Petrograd – I am so glad. It will be somewhere for us to go. A letter came from Adia this afternoon to say he is very busy with the Germans just now and cannot write as often. Ida said things are very tense in the Pistolkors household and he has issued an ultimatum that she and the children are not to go near Rasputin in the future – Aylia is in a very bad temper.

24TH NOVEMBER 1916 – THURSDAY

Today Mr and Mrs Kartzev went to lunch with her father at the Admiralty. She told me Admiral Philimore and the English Ambassador Sir George Buchanan were there. I have just come back from Uncle George's house. Ida came with me and we did a great deal of laughing. Uncle George married a Russian lady, Aunt Olga. They had moved away from Petrograd some time ago and were so pleased to see us. Our four cousins, Alexei, Maria, Helena and Misha are almost grown up. I am so glad they have come back.

Ida says that Alexander Pistolkors has gone to Helsingfors (Helsinki), where he is now attached to the staff of the General Governor of Finland, General Zeine and Aylia's temper is much improved.

27TH NOVEMBER 1916 – SUNDAY

We have been at the Admiralty all day with the children's grandfather Grigorovitch. He likes to see little Toulia dancing which she does not as well as Natasha. He gave me a small icon which he had signed on the back so I shall hang it in my room. I am making the children act out an Indian dialogue which they will do on Wednesday evening. It includes much work sewing their costumes.

30TH NOVEMBER 1916 - WEDNESDAY

Everyone seemed to be very pleased when the children had performed their Indian dialogue. The minister came and thanked me, also Mr Kartzev. May and Ida were invited and everyone was very kind to all three of us so that we had a very good time. I have heard that Nina Michaelovna and Natasha are coming home for Christmas.

1ST DECEMBER 1916 - THURSDAY

I am writing this at my desk and the children are standing nearby. They are both being punished so have taken the opportunity to scribble in my diary. The days pass so slowly when we are at home. I wish something exciting would happen. It will soon be Christmas. How time has flown by since I came here in September.

5TH DECEMBER 1916 - MONDAY

We were invited to an English whist drive. A lot of English people were present but we did not know many of them and we, Ida and I, did not play cards, we just sat talking to some old and ancient couples. It was utterly boring and I don't think we will go again. We came home in a sledge. It is the first day for them to be out.

7TH DECEMBER 1916 - WEDNESDAY

Went out in the evening to see Nina Michaelovna, who was so pleased to see me and begs me to go back to them but I could not think of it and told her so.

8TH DECEMBER 1916 – THURSDAY

Today passed without any important incidents – went out in the evening to the dress makers. Thought I would get a letter but none came – Adia says he is very busy and cannot write as often but he is still expecting a marriage ceremony when he comes back – I hear footsteps coming. I suppose Mrs Kartzev to tell me to go to bed. It is after midnight.

11TH DECEMBER 1916 – SUNDAY

At around lunchtime a call came through from Ida, asking me to meet her at the bridge early this evening to go to church – Mrs Kartzev was quite willing to let me go.

I had an awful sinking feeling as I walked towards the bridge where a car was waiting. Ida put her head out and whispered, 'It's all been arranged. I couldn't avoid it. We go to Father Gregory's after church.'

As we entered the church I saw Anna Verubova, who had sent the car, and several other ladies I knew were followers of Rasputin and when the church service was over Anna came with us in the car, chatting pleasantly about the weather. 'There's always such a peaceful and serene atmosphere with Father Gregory. All your worries will disappear as soon as you see him,' she told us. Well, neither of us felt very serene at that moment as the car stopped at the Fontanka canal. We got out on the corner of Gorokhovaya Street and walked quickly to number 64 where Rasputin lives on the third floor of a five story apartment house. In the darkness, I saw two men in long, black coats standing across the street obviously watching the house and pointed them out. 'Oh, he always has 'body-guards' outside. You see we have to make sure no harm comes to him,' Anna Verubova said as we entered the building and climbed the staircase up to his apartments. Bodyguards or police spies? Who knows. Someone took our coats in the vestibule. It was an ordinary kind of room with a huge bureau along one side, a few high backed chairs and at a table over which hung a brass chandelier shining onto glasses and plates filled with cakes, nuts and jam. The samovar steamed and there was a hum of voices. A large basket of exotic flowers stood on the table, such beautiful flowers I have never seen, especially in December. Several people, mainly women, were standing or sitting around the room. Rasputin greeted us with open arms. He looked much cleaner than I had ever seen him before; wearing a blue silk blouse and quite fat, at least fatter than in the many photographs seen in the newspapers. 'Annushka my dear,' he said, taking our hands, 'and the English ladies.' Not sure whether we were supposed to kiss his hand, we both lowered our heads and tried to avoid looking into his eyes, pretending extreme shyness. He made some peculiar signs in the air and muttered something like 'God is watching over us tonight', then in a loud voice and to the room in general he said, 'Do not believe the scandalous lies my enemies are spreading everywhere. God will punish them and they will never find redemption.'

A lady on the other side of the room started to cry, sobbing loudly. Rasputin went over to her, put his hands on her head and started to pray. After that the room went very quiet but doubt anyone could make out what he was saying – He guided her quickly into his study in an adjoining room where we could see a candle flickering under a large icon.

We sat with our glasses of tea in a corner of the room and several people, thinking we were English, remarked on our Russian speech which surprises almost everyone as we speak like natives of the country of course.

Suddenly Rasputin came out of the study, still praying and making gestures in the air. They say he is very much like a chameleon and can change character according to whoever he is with. Looking round the room with his sly, deep set eyes, in a loud voice he exclaimed 'Scandalous lies!' Ida nearly dropped her glass of tea and I, so tense, felt as though frozen to the chair. Every eye in the room was on him. 'Blessed are they that dwell in the house of the Lord,' he went on mumbling something about, 'How long will you judge unjustly and accept the wicked,' – then started to speak about his famous prophecy which has been widely publicised through many people in Petrograd, 'If I am killed, if I die at the hands of the aristocracy, then the Romanov family will also die within six months of my death – they know not, neither will they understand. They walk on in darkness.' – There was complete silence. Munya Golovina, infamous for her affair with Felix Yousoupov's brother and a devoted follower of Rasputin, led him to a seat near the table where she poured a glass of tea and some of the other women gathered around him, kneeling or sitting at his feet. He started to mumble some more prayers making the sign of the cross over the group around him on the floor.

I whispered to Ida that it was time to go and grabbing her hand, we made our way towards the door. 'Christ be with you, my dears' he said as we passed by him. We ran down the street as fast as we could go to the car waiting at the corner. Ida was already giggling as we fell into the car. I can't help thinking there will be some kind of consequences and I will be in such a lot of trouble if the Kartzevs find out. Adia would be very angry if he knew anything about it but I suppose Aylia will be pleased, not to mention the Tsarina.

All the rooms were in darkness when I got back. The house was silent; everyone had gone to bed. Such relief! Not much sleep tonight, scribbling in my diary for too long and will have nightmares about Rasputin's prophecy – no doubt.

12TH DECEMBER 1916 – MONDAY

Today Mrs Kartzev gave me a stocking filled with sweets – Everything looks very Christmas-like. I was much moved and reminded of the old times when we were all together with the family.

13TH DECEMBER 1916 – TUESDAY

In the evening went out with Ida and we had rather a lot of fun as Ida met an old acquaintance, a midshipman who is still at the naval school. He was with a friend whom he introduced to us. As soon as they knew that I was employed there by Mr Kartzev, both suddenly seemed in a great hurry to get back to the school and disappeared very quickly. It was very amusing. The 'governess' is unapproachable and most definitely 'out of bounds' you see.

14TH DECEMBER 1916 – WEDNESDAY

Stayed at home with the children. They are not at all well. In the evening went out to see Nina Michaelovna and she told me all about her stay in the south. She says I would like it there.

15TH DECEMBER 1916 – THURSDAY

We went out for a short walk. The children are better and we are invited to the children's party at Ida's place tomorrow afternoon.

16TH DECEMBER 1916 – FRIDAY

This afternoon we went in the closed motor with Andrei and Toulia to the party at Ida's – I was asked to dance – Aylia provided the Russian costume and I did the Russian dance to much applause. We played with the children and had no chance to talk. There was no mention of the supper with Rasputin which was strange I thought – but Aylia was distracted with all the children and disappeared after only a short time, leaving us to entertain them.

17TH DECEMBER 1916 – SATURDAY

We have been out twice today. It was so frosty – 15 degrees of frost. I am sitting in my room with mother's photograph just in front of me. She was so much nicer than any of us in her youth. This evening I shall pass reading.

18TH DECEMBER 1916 – SUNDAY

We have spent all day at the Admiralty with the children's grandfather. This evening I am just going to work at packing presents for the sailors – there are a great many to do and it will be late when we finish.

19TH DECEMBER 1916 – MONDAY

Again nearly all day at the Admiralty. It was the minister's younger daughter's (big Toulia) birthday – Tonight the ladies are coming to help pack the presents and I will be helping also. Everyone in the school receives a present – as well as those on service who are remembered by the Kartzevs.

We went to Ida's place for a children's party last Friday. There were two of the Grand Duke Paul's children there, that is, Princess Paley's daughters, Irene and Natalie. We tried to count how many little princes and counts were there. Also present was Count Komarovski, who is in love with Ida. There is a rumour that Rasputin has disappeared. We were so busy with the children there was hardly time to talk to anyone but a lost of whispering went on I noticed.

20TH DECEMBER 1916 – TUESDAY

It has been bitterly cold these last few days, 18 degrees of frost. Such a shock! A few days ago, the infamous Rasputin was murdered so now there will be great rejoicing amongst thousands of people. Rumours abound everywhere. I hurried over the Bridge to see Ida. She tells me it happened at the Yousoupov palace, which is very near to where she lives on the Morskaya and that Felix Yousoupov himself is somehow involved. Dmitri, son of the Grand Duke Paul by his first marriage, is thought to have fired the shots. Dmitri is a stepbrother to Alexander Pistolkors through the Grand Duke's marriage to Olga Valerianova, Princess Paley. To think that this murder happened right next to where Ida is living! There have been many people calling at her place, she says. Aylia and Anna Verubova are distraught. Pistolkors is well off the scene in Helsingfors but is expected home at any time. Aylia is inconsolable from all accounts and kneels at the icon praying and crying all the time. Yousoupov and Dmitri have been plotting to murder Rasputin for a long time and Aylia says they first gave him a great deal of poison concealed in cakes and wine, but finding it had little effect they shot him, then rolled him up in some kind of curtain and threw him from the bridge into the Neva through a hole in the ice near Petrovski Island.

As soon as his body was found the Tsarina gave orders for it to be embalmed but the body was washed and prepared for burial in the church Anna Verubova is in the process of building in

Tsarskoe Selo with the compensation money she received from the train accident. Many people think that Rasputin was her lover but we think it is more likely to be Aylia. Anna Verubova and several other women admirers of Rasputin, including Aylia, conducted a funeral service in front of the coffin. The Tsarina and her daughters placed a small icon, signed by all of them, on his chest.

Both Dmitri and Felix Yousoupov are under arrest. Prince Felix Yousoupov is descended from one of the oldest and wealthiest families in Russia and he is also related through marriage to the Tsar, having married Irena, daughter of the Tsar's sister Xenia. Dmitri and his sister Marianne were brought up by the Tsarina's sister Ella and her husband Serge, the Tsar's uncle who was assassinated in 1905. Since then Ella has become a nun and given away all her worldly possessions.

The relationships of all these people are so closely intertwined with the Romanov family. It is truly amazing to think that Rasputin was not murdered by an angry mob of the people but by one of the Romanovs themselves! The Tsarina wants both Felix Yousoupov and Dmitri Pavlovitch to be executed by firing squad – such is her anger. A lot of people think it was Dmitri Pavlovitch who shot Rasputin because Yousoupov has no army training and was always regarded as a rather effeminate playboy before his marriage.

21ST DECEMBER 1916 – WEDNESDAY

It has been such a very long day. It is nearly 1.00am and no one has gone to bed yet. Mrs Kartzev is still packing presents – every boy in the school receives a present and as there are about 700 cadets there is an awful lot of wrapping to do. We have been making Christmas cakes and dressing the trees. Today a soldier came with a letter from Adia saying he will call to take my answer back to him.

23RD DECEMBER 1916 – FRIDAY

The children are so excited by the Christmas holidays. Mrs Kartzev was extremely kind and made a real English Christmas pudding. I was almost moved to tears and reminded of my family's Christmas in England – mother would surely be making a Christmas pudding and buying presents at this time.

They say that Felix Yousoupov and Dmitri Pavlovitch are to be banished from Russia, sent abroad somewhere.

24TH DECEMBER 1916 – SATURDAY

Christmas Eve and I am tired to death. I have been making an English cake, dressing the trees – there are at least 20 Christmas trees to decorate scattered about this huge building – and all sorts of things and now it is 1.00am. I spoke to Ida by phone. She has been to a party at the Princess Paley's palace in Tsarskoe, where there was the most enormous tree in the ballroom, filled with presents and sweets for the children. They had cleared the ballroom which is used as a workroom with tables and sewing machines for making presents for the soldiers and the wounded in hospitals. Ida's three little girls had lots of presents. Prince Vladimir Paley was there, looking very handsome, with all the young girls at his feet. They had put aside their worries about Dmitri Pavlovitch for the sake of their other children, Irene and Natalie. Alexander Pistolkors escorted them. He came back home yesterday.

Today I received English newspapers from mother but don't know when I will have time to read them. We had visitors to dinner and a lot of talking. Now I am ready to cry my eyes out, I don't know why. Tonight I took a short visit to Ida and could not wait to hear her news. She also thinks it is more likely to be Dmitri Pavlovitch who shot Rasputin because of his army training.

Both Aylia and Anna Verubova are wondering what they will do without Rasputin. Princess Paley is distracted by the departure of Dmitri Pavlovitch, who has been sent to Persia despite her petitions to the Tsar. Marianne Pistolkors has also been arrested at her home where two sentries were on guard when Alexander Pistolkors went to secure her release. She went to say goodbye to Grand Duke Dmitri before his departure to Persia. I wonder whether they will ever see him again. Ida stayed there with Sandra, Olga and Tatiana alone, feeling as isolated as I am at Christmas in the midst of all the festivities throughout the holiday. Montashov, the oil millionaire, as we refer to him, thinks she is an angel. We chatted for a while, drinking tea in Ida's room and then I came home by sledge. We have been alone with the children nearly all through the holiday but it's much worse for Ida as her children see so little of their mother and she is with them night and day without a break.

25TH DECEMBER 1916 – SUNDAY

I have had many presents – a soft, warm jersey, a frame for mother's photograph and a satchel of black, watered silk – so nice. From Mrs Kartzev I had a beautiful Russian box containing a little powder box and mirror and another picture frame. The Minister Grigorovitch gave me a silver sweet dish.

I was asked many times to dance the Russian dance again so had to change quickly into the costume. I had much applause. Now I am very tired.

26TH DECEMBER 1916 – MONDAY

I went to see Nina Michaelovna and Natasha at their house. They are here for the holidays. We played the gramophone and as in the days of old danced around the tree. Petya watched. He says he is too old to dance! Nina Michaelovna and Natasha were so pleased to see me. She talked a lot about their stay in the South also of days long past when I first went to work for her. Now she wants me to go back with them to Tiflis but that is quite out of the question.

I have written to Adia. The soldier he sent will collect it tomorrow.

27TH DECEMBER 1916 – TUESDAY

We went to another Christmas Tree Party with the children and then more visitors came for dinner in the evening and so we were on best behaviour. It has been such a long day and tonight I will cry myself to sleep.

31ST DECEMBER 1916 – SATURDAY

At last I managed to get away to see Ida. She is surrounded by the aftermath of Rasputin's murder – Aylia and her sister Anna mourning his death. It all happened so suddenly just before Christmas. I still can't believe it. I was so occupied with the children and their parties and presents. It is such a lonely time for us at Christmas. Well, at least there will be one less thing to worry about now that Rasputin is out of the way. Although we were curious, I must admit we were dreading the supper with him in case we had to kiss his hand. Little did I think he would be dead in less than a week. Most of the population are rejoicing now he's gone. I can't help wondering whether his prophecy about the Tsar will turn out to be true. In spite of all the upset about Rasputin Ida still received her Christmas card from the Tsarina, Signed in English 'to Miss Ida with greeting and best wishes – Alexandra'. It is an English postcard of a sentry, with busby and sword, in the Royal Scots Greys 2nd Dragoons, of which the Tsar is Colonel in Chief. It is proudly displayed on Ida's desk. She has a wonderful signature with a great big flourish on the 'A' in Alexandra.

Petia – Miss Daisy – Natasha – Nina Michaelovna-Lukina

Petia – Natasha – Piotr Petrovitch-Lukin

Miss Daisy with Natasha and Petia

Natasha in dance costume

Postcard from Arcadi Dmitrich, a soldier in the Imperial Russian Horse Guards Regiment, 1916

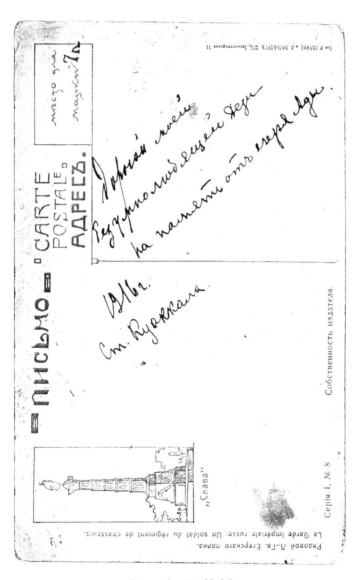

'Remember Kuokkola'

The Admiralty, Petrograd

Naval Minister, Ivan Constantin Grigorovitch (signed)

Director of Naval College, Kartzev

Kartzev family (in Finland)
Natalia (Little Toulia) – Mrs Kartzev – Andre – Natalia (Big Toulia)

The Naval College (left), looking across the Lieutenant Schmidt bridge, Vasilevski Island

*Naval Minister Ivan Constantin Grigorovitch with the Tsar Nicholas II at the
Naval Monument*

Miss Ida with Sandra, Olga, and Tatiana Pistolkors

Anna Verubova in wheelchair with Tatiana, Sandra and Ida in Tsarskoe Selo

Miss Ida with the Tsarina in Tsarskoe Selo, 1916. The Tsarina is wearing her nurse's uniform head dress

Alexander Pistolkors, son of Princess Paley

Aylia Pistolkors

Aylia Pistolkors wearing her diamond tiara

Father Gregory – Rasputin

Madame Souvorin, wife of the editor of the Novoe Vremia in Russian costume

Princess Paley with children

Anna Verubova

Grand Duchess Olga, youngest sister of the Tsar, with Sandra in Tsarskoe Selo

English postcard from the Tsarina, signed to Miss Ida, 1916. The Tsar was Colonel-in-Chief of this regiment – The Royal Scots Greys.

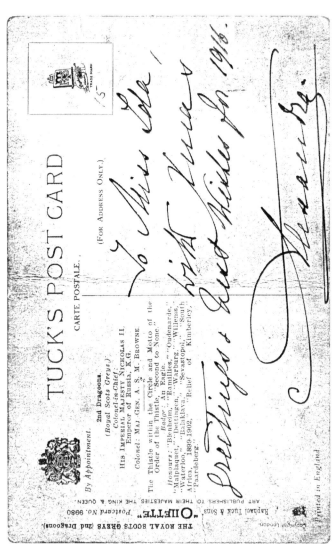

Postcard back
Christmas Greetings to Miss Ida from the Tsarina

Grand Duchess Maria (signed), 3rd daughter of the Tsar

The Pistolkors children with Cossack guard in Tsarscoe Selo

The Pistolkors' apartments, Morskaya Prospect, first floor

Meeting at Rasputin's apartment. Far left Alexander Pistolkors and Aylia

Vava and May

May, Vava and Mrs Sartisson, 1912

The Sartisson house and estate, Terijoki, Finland

The Dickinson family in St Petersburg, 1902. Left to Right: Frances Ann, Ella, May, Vara, Ida, Leslie, Alexander Francis, Daisy

1917

It was Natasha's birthday but I did not go. Also it was Andrei's birthday and how happy he was! He had very many presents. I wish I was a child again to be free of all cares and worries of this life.

They say the Tsar is coming back from the army headquarters in Mogiliev. I wonder what can possibly happen then. He has been Tsar for 22 years. No news from anyone.

6TH JANUARY 1917 − FRIDAY

Today has been a holiday and so very dull. Andrei had his lesson on the violin from a sailor who is the first violin in the school orchestra − and is a very good violinist. I stayed to watch. He is also learning some carpentry and we have a whole set of gymnastic equipment put up so now we can swing on ropes and do all kinds of exercises. As I was always known as the tomboy of the family when I was young, maybe I will dare to do some exercises as well. It will at least relieve the monotony. If Mr Kartzev sees me, oh my goodness, he would no doubt be very shocked and tell me it is not appropriate behaviour for his son's governess. No letters are coming through. Adia is not writing very often now.

I am very tired tonight but will try to learn a little of the 3rd Psalm before Mrs Kartzev comes home.

Repeat after me: *Lord, how are they increased that trouble me! Many are they that rise up against me.* Before the end of next week the children have to learn this until they are word perfect. *I cried unto the Lord with my voice and he heard me out of his holy hill. I laid me down and slept. I awakened, for the Lord sustained me.*

Maybe I will go to sleep now. The house is silent.

11TH JANUARY 1917 – WEDNESDAY

We have been at the Admiralty today. There were some English admirals and generals having lunch there who had just arrived from England and it made me feel very homesick just looking at them. In the evening I spoke with Mr and Mrs Kartzev until about 2.00am. We discussed the awful state of affairs in town and Rasputin's murder and the government. Popular hatred seems to focus on the Tsar, in fact all the Romanov family but no evidence is found that Rasputin was a paid German spy, only they say he was against the war. Mr Kartzev wonders what Ida is going to do. He says she is in great danger there, even more so now that Rasputin is dead. His death is seen as a great triumph by thousands of people, according to news reports.

14TH JANUARY 1917 – SATURDAY

There is some kind of blockade which means I will have no more letters from England. Today I have been making an English cake which takes about six hours to make and four more to cook. There is still some flour available in the school kitchens but queues for bread are everywhere in town. This evening went to see Ida, over the bridge and onto the Morskaya. Mr Forrest, the head chauffeur, was there. He is English, married to a Russian lady named Olga who is very nice and they have a son named Shura about 5 years old. Mrs Forrest has invited us to a musical evening at her house. She plays the piano and has a beautiful singing voice. The Montashov brothers were outside on the pavement and bid us a very elaborate good evening.

15TH JANUARY 1917 – SUNDAY

Today we were up in the school. There was a lottery for the war effort and saw a lot of the boys who look very smart in their uniforms. I am reading a book called *The Virginians.*

20TH JANUARY 1917 – FRIDAY

Went to Ida's place. There were many visitors including an artist who paints Aylia's portrait. When tea was served, Aylia asked the artist if he would be kind enough to walk around all the ladies and choose what he considered to be their best feature, on the face that is! It was so embarrassing for us, though Aylia seemed to enjoy it very much. He looked at each one of us for a long time, very seriously, and we couldn't help giggling. Ida, of course, was flirting with him, turning her face this way and that. He chose my ears in the end, believe it or not! How flattering! And Ida's chin which she displayed from every angle was chosen after much giggling.

She had been to Tsarskoe Selo where Princess Paley is anxiously awaiting news of her step-son Dmitri. Anna Verubova is still mourning the death of Rasputin. Her house is filled with even more flowers placed around a photograph of 'Father Gregory'. The Tsarina, who has aged so much these last few months, knows little of what is happening in Petrograd, that people are hailing as heroes both Dmitri and Felix Yousoupov. Dmitri, one of her favourites as a child, was brought up by her sister Ella and at one time was considered to be an eligible husband for her eldest daughter Olga. Under the influence of Felix, they both became outrageous playboys in the nightlife of Petersburg's bars and cafés so the proposed engagement to Olga was called off. Anna Verubova gave Ida a photograph of Rasputin as a remembrance of 'Our Friend'. Ida says she will hide it, since it is in rather a nice frame, in case Pistolkors sees it. Does Anna Verubova really expect her to hang it in her room? But since it is in the most beautiful oval frame, she can hardly dispose of it.

23RD JANUARY 1917 – MONDAY

It was so cold today when we went out for a walk. I got my cheek frozen and was reminded of our father's tales about the Russian winters of his childhood, when he told us that if you spit out, it is frozen solid before it hits the ground. I wonder what is happening in England. I rubbed snow onto my cheek very hard but it was still frozen.

24TH JANUARY 1917 – TUESDAY

It is nearly 5.00pm. The day has passed as usual. I am making some bread for Mrs Kartzev.

25TH JANUARY 1917 – WEDNESDAY

We went out for a walk but it was so cold we came home very quickly. I have no news from Adia. A letter from May came to say they are thinking of going to Nijni Novgorod and Mrs Sartisson wants to know if I would like to go with them and find another post there or give English lessons. They think the food question is better in Nijni.

30TH JANUARY 1917 – MONDAY

We got up very early this morning to have coffee with Mr and Mrs Kartzev as it is his birthday today. The children wished him Happy Birthday before he disappeared into his office.

Andrei is with the carpenter just now making a terrible noise and Toulia is gluing pictures into a book. I really do not know how much longer I can remember to keep scribbling into my diary. A whole day spent in the house. I do wish the war would end and we could all go back to England to see mother and father. How hopeless it seems to wish for impossibilities.

31ST JANUARY 1917 – TUESDAY

In the afternoon Admiral Jerome came to our house. It is Mr Kartzev's Names Day so the minister Grigorovitch came to dinner and we had to be on scene with our best behaviour. I had wanted to go out in the evening but dinner was so late and the children were late to bed. I had to cancel it.

1ST FEBRUARY 1917 – WEDNESDAY

Time is passing just as usual. It is 5.00pm. I will go out tonight with Ida and we will call in a café and forget all the worries and woes for an hour or two I hope. Most of the cafés have gypsy music playing and are quite lively with lots of soldiers and people.

9TH FEBRUARY 1917 – THURSDAY

It is just 8.30pm and I have come to my room. It has gone very quiet outside but I do not want to read and just keep thinking about going back to England. It is true we are getting good wages but the rate of exchange is going down and things are so expensive. A piece of soap is 2 roubles 50 kopeks and new boots nothing less than 100 roubles. After the war, we shall perhaps have a good, long holiday. Trouble in the streets in expected – not allowed out with the children.

10TH/11TH FEBRUARY 1917 – FRIDAY/SATURDAY

Nothing of note. Have been baking bread and making an English cake. Two whole days spent indoors.

12TH FEBRUARY 1917 – SUNDAY

The weather has changed, gone much warmer. A soldier brought a letter from Adia. I have to send back an answer on 16th.

13TH FEBRUARY 1917 – MONDAY

Toulia and Andrei are not well – we are staying indoors. Trouble expected in the streets again. I wish the war was over. How hopeless it seems to wait so long to see our mother and father. Shut indoors all day and no fresh air and Miss Daisy, Miss Daisy ringing in my ears.

14TH FEBRUARY 1917 – TUESDAY

We were at home all day. Nothing of note to write about. I wrote a letter to Adia.

16TH FEBRUARY 1917 – THURSDAY

The soldier has not been to collect the letter for Adia. Toulia swallowed a button and gave me such a fright. She is very naughty and thought she would die.

19TH FEBRUARY 1917 – SUNDAY

We have been at the Admiralty the whole day with the children's grandfather.

I cannot dare to think very far ahead. This summer both May and Ida will be away and how lonely it will be without them.

20TH FEBRUARY 1917 – MONDAY

Went to see my pupil Veronica. Posted letter to Adia. He writes very little these days.

22ND FEBRUARY 1917 – WEDNESDAY

It was Mrs Kartzev's birthday. I am so glad we are going out. It makes the day pass more quickly.

23RD FEBRUARY 1917 – THURSDAY

Went over the bridge to see Ida but she had gone to Tsarskoe Selo – I expect she took the children to see Anna Verubova. There is no news from England. I cannot think why Ida has been summoned to visit at Tsarskoe Selo – in the midst of all this chaos. Perhaps they want to know what is happening in town – also to see the children. They are expecting the Tsar to return very soon now. Everything is so very secret these days with people escaping by various routes out of Petersburg – and taking their money with them.

25TH FEBRUARY 1917 – SATURDAY

As there is trouble in the streets we are not going out. It makes the day seem so long. The soldiers are everywhere and two or three times a day we see the Cossacks rushing past. All the bridges are guarded and they say the strikes are just as bad as in 1905. I should like to see what is going on but am not allowed out. Cannons are to be used if the trouble does not stop. I am just glad some of those horrible merchants who have been raising the price of food will suffer. The government is to blame for that, I am sure. Some people are saying the Germans are behind all the strikes as it will give them a better chance to win the war.

I had a letter from Adia, who says he has not heard from me for a month but it is not true. I have sent several letters.

26TH FEBRUARY 1917 – SUNDAY

Today the streets are much worse and thousands of young girls and boys about 14 to 15 years old are marching and crowded everywhere. All the tramcars are stopped. Not been out.

27TH FEBRUARY 1917 – MONDAY

Again at home and time passes so slowly. I would like to go out to visit Ida as it is only a 20 minute walk over the bridge to the Morskaya. I am not at all afraid of the crowds. After all, there is only one end for each of us and if mine comes sooner do not mind as one day drags after another.

20TH MARCH 1917 – MONDAY

I am still alive but it is a great wonder. It seems so long since I wrote anything down 'til now when I can perhaps describe what has happened to us.

On February 27th the children were put to bed ready dressed because there was such chaos on the streets. All our windows look out onto the quay, so from time to time I went peeping through and saw crowds of people running towards the bridge where they managed to take control from the soldiers. No soldiers could pass. The cannons were going off and there was a lot of shooting. At intervals troops of Cossacks on horseback would race past like lightning and all the crowd would scatter. Stray bullets started to come through the windows lodging in pictures and the walls. The next time I looked out I could see that a lot of the soldiers had started to join the mob of people and were even shooting their own officers who would not give in to the revolutionaries.

I was quite terrified but tried to stay calm for the sake of the children. Mrs Kartzev had gone to see her father at the Admiralty before the worst of the fighting had started and she could not get back. Mr Kartzev was in his study, making telephone calls. At about 3.00am he came to tell me that he had been into the school where he made a speech to the 700 cadets, telling them not to fire if the soldiers camc but also not to give up their rifles and ammunition. He had put some of the boys on guard to give the alarm if they came. I watched the troops pass with a mob of revolutionaries following them. The night dragged on and for some reason I suddenly thought of hiding all the silver, costly vases and valuables in Mrs Kartzev's bathroom where I hid them in a recess under the bath. The children woke every now and then and asked for me. All the servants were huddled together in a corner of the staircase, praying very loudly to a thousand saints and they would not move, even after requests from Mr Kartzev.

At about 5.00am Mr Kartzev came rushing into the room. 'They are here,' he shouted and told me to take the children and run out through the yards at the back of the building to Dr Kazanski's (the school doctor) as quickly as I could. 'We are surrounded by machine guns,' he said.

The worst of it was that I did not know the way because the yards are like twisting corridors and I had never left the building in this way before. As we were leaving I saw Ivan, the man who looks after the stoves and begged him to show us the way. I was carrying Toulia and dragging Andrei along by the hand, both of them whimpering and very frightened. It was so slippery I could hardly get along and suddenly realised that I was wearing my slippers.

We had hardly left the building when I heard a rumbling sound growing louder and louder – soldiers' boots I suppose, then all at once shooting started with bullets flying everywhere. I knew they must be trying to surround the building. Just as we were about to turn into another space, some of the soldiers came running towards us and stopped Ivan but none of them touched us and we continued on our way until we saw another two soldiers running in our direction but they dropped almost at our feet, shot dead, one of them through the head. We had to step over them to go past. The boys in the school somewhere must have been firing at them.

At last we staggered into the kitchen of Doctor Kazanski. He hurried us through the house and into his bathroom where there were no windows and there we sat all the next day without any food listening to the shooting outside. The soldiers had already searched his place and taken every last morsel of food.

At about 9 o'clock that evening (28th February), a sailor came to the house who was the servant's boyfriend. He was on service but also in the Naval School and had seen all the day's turmoil. He told us that at about 5.00am the soldiers had broken in and demanded rifles. Some of the oldest boys, the midshipmen, started to shoot at them from a hidden place. At this, the soldiers were very angry and both sides started firing. All the lower ranks and younger boys joined the soldiers. They ransacked the school's kitchen, took all the food and then made their way to our apartment where they arrested Mr Kartzev.

The sailor said they had left the place in a terrible mess, cut many of the paintings, damaged the furniture and cut off the telephone. When they took poor Mr Kartzev, he said, 'Do what you will with me but please do not harm the boys.' The sailor said they had eaten all our food as well. They were searching all the time for the midshipmen who had fired on them, when someone told them these boys were hiding in the attics so all the doors were left open to let them pass in and out of the rooms. They searched all day but without success because it is such an enormous building. Then they threatened to blow up the whole place if they did not come out, so in the end the boys had to give themselves up. I do not know what happened to them. Maybe they were shot.

We lived for four days in the Doctor's bathroom, having just sips of water and a few crumbs of dry bread. On the third day Mrs Kartzev arrived with her sister Toulia. They had walked across the frozen river from the Admiralty amidst all the shooting. She went out of her mind when told that Mr Kartzev had been arrested and she had to be held down on the bathroom floor to stop her rushing out. All the four days we were there, soldiers were entering the house without warning searching for rifles. On the fourth day they found the Doctor's rifle and revolver and then took him to the Duma where he had to sign a paper to say he was on the side of the Revolution.

That evening I fainted away for several hours and they could not bring me round. When I opened my eyes both children were crying and my first thought was that their father had been shot. One of the servants found some old coffee from somewhere and forced me to drink it. The children thought I was going to die.

Later that morning, soldiers came in, found us in the bathroom and said we were under arrest. We were marched off through the back yards and passages into the school cellars, a terrible place like a big dungeon where about 10 women were lying or sitting on the stone floor. Sailors were on guard, their swords unsheathed, some with bayonets who stared at us with great mistrust and hatred. The room was stinking to high heaven and very dark. In one corner was a kind of open drain with a makeshift wooden screen, which was used for a lavatory. No one was allowed to leave and the other people looked terrified.

We remained on that cold, stone floor for the next six days. They brought porridge and cabbage to us once a day and by the second or third day we all began to look yellow. The children, poor things, sat there bewildered, hearing all the bad language and one day two women fought viciously over some spilt cabbage. I have no idea who these people were. Some of them did not seem like anti-revolutionaries and kept their distance with as much mistrust as the sailors. They were all starving of course. We had heard that all the prisons had been opened and many convicts had joined the Red Guards but those who refused to fight were either shot or imprisoned again. Whatever their crimes, most of these looked like murderers and prostitutes.

Mrs Kartzev was quite dazed, praying all the time for her husband, whilst the elder Toulia prayed for her father.

Scrambling my brains somehow, I told stories to the children and tried to get them to sleep. On the sixth day I was beginning to think death would be a blessing. I told Mrs Kartzev I would not sit there any longer since I have a British passport and am therefore a British subject and they could not keep me imprisoned.

At this they all started crying again and clinging to me. Mrs Kartzev begged me on bended knees not to leave her with the three children. In the end, I promised I would return to them as soon as I found out what had happened to my sisters. When the guards changed I had noticed a sailor whom I recognised. He was one of the men who had worked on our gymnasium four months ago, so approached him and gave him to understand that whoever was responsible for keeping me imprisoned would pay the penalty. He looked quite confused at my angry words, but shrugged his shoulders and said that he was only obeying orders. I told him he must take me to whoever was in charge or there would be trouble. When I turned round all the others were staring at me as if I had gone mad. Mrs Kartzev kept asking me why I had done it, why I had spoken so crossly, why I had shouted. 'We will be shot,' she said, then subsided into utter dejection. My heart felt like a stone.

That afternoon the same sailor came to take me to those who were now in command of the Naval School. I followed him through the endless corridors until we reached a door where two soldiers stood on guard. The sailor told them who I was and one of them jerked a thumb at the door. There was nothing military about these soldiers. The Red Guard consists mainly of ordinary workmen. At first I could hardly see anything after being in the dark for so long and the room was thick with tobacco smoke. I went towards a table at the far end where four men sat. At the head of the table stood a young officer whom I recognised, though his clothes were tattered and torn and his epaulettes gone. He was one of the officers who taught English at the school. He made no sign of knowing me but asked in English what I wanted. I replied in English that I had no need of an interpreter, especially one who was licking the boots of those around him. I was well past caring after six days spent in that grim dungeon. Then I spoke to the other four who seemed taken aback at my Russian speech. I asked to telephone my sister, explaining that she also was a British subject and that people would be searching for me. They decided, after some muttering, to let me do this provided I spoke no English. Before I left the room they asked what I had said to the officer in English and told me that if I did not answer truthfully they would take away my permission to use the phone. I told the truth and they roared with laughter. The officer just glared at me.

As I was leaving, another officer from the school came in. He had been Mr Kartzev's adjutant and spoke English quite well. He saluted me and turned to the men at the table giving a big wink, then at the door took my hand as though he was a very old acquaintance of mine, whispering that he was only trying to save his wife and children.

I walked again down the corridor between two guards with open bayonets. They had been ordered to shoot me if I spoke one word of English or said where I was calling from. I was trembling from head to foot by this time in case I let slip a word of English when speaking to May.

May was frantic with questions. 'Where are you? Speak in English to me.' I was only able to tell her I was safe. I was so nervous and thought afterwards that the call had been quite useless.

When I got back to the dungeon I found the children in hysterics, thinking I had gone forever. To calm them we tried to say prayers with them.

Quite early next morning there was a loud noise of shouting out orders. One of the guards came up to us, said we were released and could go. We made our way out into the daylight in a complete daze. Where could we go? Our apartments were occupied and Mrs Kartzev would not hear of going back to Doctor Kazanski so we decided to walk across the river to the Admiralty where she thought her father might give us some kind of protection.

It was very frosty and icy cold in the early morning sunshine. All the people in the street were wearing red ribbons on their hats and coats, while some went past shouting, 'Down with the Tsar.' We managed to pick up from the pavement a piece of ribbon which someone had dropped and made our way out onto the ice of the river. Our legs were so stiff from sitting and we were so weak from lack of food, we began slipping and falling over. I had only my thin slippers, the others had boots. We made a joke of this out of desperation for the children's sake and suddenly we were all laughing. The sun was shining and the ice shone like a thousand diamonds almost blinding us. It was so dazzling after the darkness we had just emerged from, we had to shade our eyes. It felt so good to be free. There was no traffic, no sledges and a lot of the dead people had not been taken away.

Half sliding and crawling, we made our way slowly over the ice to the Admiralty. Ivan Grigorovitch was still free and a lot of people wanted him to remain minister, however he said we could not possibly stay there. The soldiers could come back to arrest him at any moment but he said we must wash and have something to eat. My feet were almost frozen so he asked one of the servants to find me some socks and galoshes.

As we were eating a troop of soldiers arrived with Alexander Kerenski at their head. We were so afraid we would be arrested again but he walked very calmly into the room, shook hands with Grigorovitch and made a point of shaking hands with each of us. What a surprise that was! He is leader of the Provisional Government which has replaced the previous one. He makes very moving, impassioned speeches to the people and the troops. He spoke in a loud voice to the minister, saying we must make ourselves at home just as before and that he only required the use of two or three rooms. When he knew I was from England he smiled and spoke some English words, saying we should not be afraid and that no harm would come to us. I must say, his English was very good.

There was no time to tell him what we had just been through. It would have been pointless when hundreds are lying dead in the streets and I could hardly speak. I know that a lot of soldiers wept when he made speeches at the front. After all, he was once a lawyer and his power is only in words.

The soldiers had started to search again so Mrs Kartzev kissed her father goodbye and he told us to go to Admiral Bostrem's house where he thought we would be safe. The children hugged and kissed him until tears came into his eyes. He thanked me for staying with the children.

Once again we crossed the river and as we were nearing the other side we saw soldiers shooting at some officers. None of the bullets touched us though they were very close. We could not leave the pathway we were on as the snow was piled high on each side and we were obliged to pass the soldiers. As we approached I shouted at them to stop firing. They turned to stare at me and I think it was little Toulia in her red coat and with some red ribbon in her hair who caught their attention. As we walked past one of the soldiers remarked, 'The little lady is in the height of fashion.' Mrs Kartzev said how lucky it was that we had chosen red for the colour of her winter coat.

Admiral Bostrem was not really a very good friend of the Kartzev family or the minister. Some years earlier he had been discharged because of some mistake he had made. They had not been on such good terms since then, although the children were always invited to Christmas parties there. He had four sons who were attending the Naval School. Mrs Bostrem tried to make us welcome but the children were very tired and irritable and I could see quite plainly that they were ill. That evening we called the doctor who diagnosed chickenpox and he said there was an epidemic.

We were isolated immediately in a large nursery, windows darkened and just a little night lamp burning which I placed as far from the window as possible to avoid attracting the attention of the huge bands of soldiers who were searching all the houses for rifles. We three were then in quarantine from the rest of the family. The room was far away from their living quarters. It was full of toys, children's desks and a big tank of tropical fish. I found some paper and pencils in one of the desks and once the children were asleep tried to write down what had happened as I was quite unable to sleep.

Mrs Kartzev received news that her husband had attacked one of the sailors who was guarding him. The sailor was armed and Mr Kartzev was badly wounded in three places during the fight. He was taken to the prison hospital, so she went to see if she could get permission to visit him and move him to a private hospital. Before she got there, he had asked for paper and pencil to write a letter from his bed. Then, with the point of the pencil at his temple, he had rushed at the wall embedding the pencil quite deeply in his forehead. Another operation had then been performed to remove the lead and he was lying very ill and weak swathed in bandages when she arrived.

After a great deal of trouble, Mrs Kartzev managed to have him removed to a private hospital where she was allowed to stay with him all the time. She came here every other day to see how the children were and during that time was mostly wondering how Mr Kartzev was coping without her. The children seem to be quite forgotten, almost an afterthought. They never ask for her. Their affection is all centred on me, the one who is with them night and day. Even the elder Toulia pushes little notes under the door every day because she is alone with people she hardly knows. Such sad, little notes she writes about her mother and how she died. She begs me to take her to England if her father is killed because she does not want to stay with her sister and hates her brother-in-law.

One of the servants who brings our food is called Dunia. She informed me that any requests or orders would be ignored in future because the new government says it is her turn to make demands, so she is asking for more money. She wears a red ribbon on her blouse and is always going to 'meetings'. She is very talkative, relating news of the household from day to day. I think she pitied me because I did not eat much or ask her to do anything. Yesterday she even came in with a duster but did not use it.

Reading and singing to the children passed some of the day, then I had to powder them with calamine every so often to stop them scratching. The nights seemed so long as I walked about the room. At one end was a large aquarium, now full of dead fish floating on top of the water. I think the darkened room and lack of food have finished them off. We were disturbed several times by soldiers searching for rifles and the doctor left a sleeping tablet which I was afraid to take. The Minister Grigorovitch sent a man over every day to see how we were.

Last night whilst I was writing, I heard footsteps and voices in the next room which is a large reception room, so I hid my scribbling inside a desk. An officer came in with about 12 or 15 soldiers behind him. I spoke the usual phrase, 'We have no rifles here, only two sick children.'

He stared into the room, grabbed the lamp and brought it close to my face then turning to the men told them to order the servants to make tea. He said, 'We will rest here until morning.' Then he closed the door. By this time I had recognised him as one of the soldiers who used to drill on the quay and as we passed, he always made a salute as if I was an old acquaintance. One day he made a direct stop in front of us in such a way that I had to shake hands with him. He asked if he could walk with us but I said we were doing lessons whilst we walked and could not interrupt them.

He announced in a grand voice that I was now his prisoner. He began to walk round the room and said he thought I would be just the person he had been looking for.

'Looking for?' I asked.

'Yes, to live on my estate in the South, to take care of my children.'

All at once I saw little Andrei moving towards us. He had untied the icon from the head of his bed and was holding it aloft, looking quite pitiful with his red-spotted face.

'Please do not take our Miss Daisy away from us, for God's sake, because we have no one to look after us except for her.'

The officer told him he must go back to bed but he just stood there waving the icon and refused to move.

I managed to steer him back to the bed and told the officer that we were all very ill and needed a drink of water but he sat down, smiling to himself and asked in a sarcastic way if I thought he would make a good nurse. He then started to tell me how much I would like living in the South, how no one would ever find me, that we governesses were 'all convention' which I would soon lose after living with him in the South.

I tried to think how I could escape. I thought of bribing Dunia to sit with the children or trying to telephone May. He sat there, obviously enjoying the situation until the early hours of the morning, telling me how his wife had died and how he was going to leave the army. I think he was in the Finnish Guards, stationed near to us on the 13th Line. He had a Polish accent and looked about 35. His first name was Kirill. As time went on, he became more and more amorous and I became more and more afraid, until suddenly more soldiers arrived and he rounded up his men and went out saying he would return very soon.

I decided to write a note to May and place it in one of the desks. Perhaps I should go to the Consul but how silly it would sound. I wrote his name on the note and one line: *He intends to take me to his estate somewhere in the south. Please ask Arcardi*

Dmitritch to look for me. All the next day I tried to think what I could do. I could not leave the children and Dunia was not a person to be trusted. My thoughts kept drifting back to last summer in Kuokkola with the Loukin family and Adia. How much I missed them. How far away it all seemed.

In the late afternoon Mrs Kartzev arrived to say we were moving to another place near the Nicholas station. Thank God! I am terrified in case the dreadful Polish officer comes back. It is only a temporary lodging. We had been in the nursery room for ten whole days. I think it may be more but I lost count.

21ST MARCH 1917 - TUESDAY

We are still at the Bostrem's. It is simply awful to sit in the house all day. Nothing is settled yet.

22ND MARCH 1917 - WEDNESDAY

Managed to get out to see Ida and what chaotic scenes met me there. Most of the servants have run away leaving Ida alone in one room with the three girls who are also ill with chickenpox.

Pistolkors was arrested in Helsingfors (Helsinki) and is in prison. Aylia packed up her things and dressed as a peasant in wide skirts and boots ran off before all the trouble started, taking all her precious jewellery and diamond tiara sewn into her skirts and the lining of her coat. She is trying to get to Copenhagen or Stockholm but no one knows where she is or who she has gone with. Just like me Ida has been left with the children, Sandra, Olga and Tatiana who are all very ill, especially the youngest one. Ida cannot leave them. Mr Forrest, the chauffeur, has been bringing food for them as their kitchens were ransacked as well.

It is pathetic to see the three little girls, Tatiana crying very loudly and their mother nowhere in sight. No one knows what it is like to be locked into a room with three sick children day and night for so long a time. The doctor calls every four or five days and otherwise there is no diversion. Ida was so glad to see me she burst into tears.

It was a great surprise to hear that Aylia had gone. Even Ida did not know until the last moment as it was all kept very secret for fear the servants would find out and the children would be upset. She says that Anna Verubova might have been taken away and imprisoned in the Peter and Paul Fortress, according to rumours she has heard. The oil millionaire Montashov has stood guard outside her room with a revolver, repeating the same phrase: 'We have no rifles, only three sick children in here.' Ida seems to have grown very close to him as he was quite prepared to die in order to protect them, a very brave man.

Anna Verubova and all the family of the Tsar have been arrested and are under guard at the Alexander Palace. The Tsar, they say, will abdicate. In Tsarskoe Selo, the Tsarina's daughters and Anna have had chickenpox as well. On Sunday 19th March, May went away to Nijni Novgorod. I have no news of Adia. Toulia, the minister's second daughter, has gone to her father today.

I am so tired of everything, so tired.

24TH MARCH 1917 – FRIDAY

The Tsar has abdicated. No one seems to know what is happening. Today was the day when all the dead were buried, that is the people who died for the Revolution. All the people had a holiday and the streets were in such an awful state, thousands crowded in the sleet and wet.

This is the end of the sixth week of Lent. How near Easter is.

The children are a little better. Another day spent in the house. Tomorrow we are moving to a place near the Nicholas station, to a friend of the Kartzevs. Ida is going away to Helsingfors with the children to see Pistolkors. Something to do with money I think, as the message she sent was coded and in English so only I could understand it. He was arrested by some drunken soldiers in Helsingfors who tore off his epaulettes and hit him with the butts of their rifles, driving him out onto a public open square to be shot. He was the eleventh out of nineteen men made to stand in a semi-circle. When the fifth man had been shot, a car filled with naval officers their arms tied behind their backs arrived and the mob of soldiers turned on these men with their rifles and bayonets and tore them to pieces. Whilst the fighting was going on another soldier herded the remaining fourteen men including Pistolkors, who were still standing in the square, back into the prison dungeons. They were saved from the fury of the mob. A few days later, Pistolkors managed to escape.

Newspaper descriptions of these dreadful scenes in Helsingfors were published but no one knew anything about Pistolkors, until a telegram arrived from the Commissary for Finland saying, 'The corpse of Pistolkors has not been found.' After his escape, I don't know how, he came back to Petrograd and joined the British Tank Corps. Wearing British officer's uniform and under the command of Colonel Locker Lampson, he then returned to Helsingfors. He is a very experienced soldier who has been lucky to survive the war and the Revolution, so far.

We now have a provisional government under Kerenski but no one knows what is going on as there is chaos everywhere. There is still some shooting in the streets and general disorder.

I am alone now and will be alone for Easter without my sisters. Feeling so lonely.

29TH MARCH 1917 – WEDNESDAY

A very dull, monotonous day. In the evening I went out to say goodbye to Ida and felt very sad coming home. We moved to a little house that belongs to a friend of Mrs Kartzev and I have been to the school for some of my things. The rooms are in a dreadful mess – broken furniture and bullet holes everywhere, broken glass from the windows underfoot and looking so deserted and bitterly cold. I found some of the silver and the precious vases under the bath, untouched.

30TH MARCH 1917 – THURSDAY

This evening the bell rang and I nearly jumped out of my skin as it was Adia. He did not stay long. He wanted to see me but I could not. I was too upset and tired. How he has managed to find me, I do not know!

31ST MARCH 1917 – FRIDAY

We were busy all day with the children, painting eggs and making *paska*. Adia rang twice but I could not see him. Went to the school to change my things.

1ST APRIL 1917 – SATURDAY

We were occupied painting eggs again. Saw Adia for a few minutes in the afternoon. He is just the same. I will see him tomorrow perhaps. He wants to marry before the autumn. He may go to France or to the south of Russia the next time he goes to war. I have no emotions left.

2ND APRIL 1917 – SUNDAY

Khristos Voskres!

This was Easter Day, how different from last year. We did not go to church. I had some presents.

Friends of the Kartzevs called. I wish we had a place to live. It is rotten to live like this. What is going to be the end of our wanderings I do not know. Mrs Kartzev spends most of her time at the hospital where Mr Kartzev is feeling better but the wound in his head is still bad.

4TH APRIL 1917 – TUESDAY

Adia is furious because I will not agree to marry before the autumn and goes away sulking for a few days before he turns up again.

7TH APRIL 1917 – FRIDAY

The children are going out for a short walk today for the first time. That is all.

9TH APRIL 1917 – SUNDAY

Ida rang to say that she is back from Helsingfors and will stay here for some time. I am so glad. She had a very nice time there, staying in a hotel. Pistolkors wants her to take the children to Sweden. She is afraid to go by herself but this is the only way possible to get the children out of Petrograd and reunited with their mother; that is if she can get her papers signed and passport in order. Even so, it's a very long journey with three small children. She is not very keen on living in Sweden with them so I do not know what will happen or where she will go from there.

10TH APRIL 1917 – MONDAY

Today, as I was going to the hospital with the children, we saw a general shot by some soldiers. We hurried past as he was carried into a house. Truly awful scenes! The people on the streets are in a very excited state, some for making peace and the others for finishing the war. A lot of angry demonstrations are going on and processions all day, from morning 'til night – no cars.

16TH APRIL 1917 – SUNDAY

The children have been ill with nettle fever. I suppose this trouble has made them very nervous, poor things and they see very little of their mother. Adia is very angry that I cannot see him every day. I have not been out.

17TH APRIL 1917 – MONDAY

There are processions on the streets from morning to night again. No tramcars are running and no one is working. I do not feel very well so will not venture out. As I am writing my hands are so cold I can hardly hold the pen. There is no fuel for the stoves.

20TH APRIL 1917 – THURSDAY

Everything upset again with shooting on the streets. There are two parties, one for peace and one for war and another for ending the war. They are fighting it out.

21ST APRIL 1917 – FRIDAY

Sitting in the house feeling very anxious most of the time about all the row going on outside, wondering which side will win. Very noisy meetings all over the place and tonight there may be some kind of decision. I am getting used to the shooting. Tonight there will be some kind of decision.

22ND APRIL 1917 – SATURDAY

An order came out this morning that everything must be stopped, no more meetings or demonstrations to be held. It seems the war will continue. I must try to get out and find a dentist as my teeth need attention very badly now. I have toothache all the time.

23RD APRIL 1917 – SUNDAY

Went with the children to the hospital to see their father and mother.

This evening I went to see Ida and found Adia there. How strange everything seems to be. Of course, if he cannot have me he will find someone else I suppose.

Just now there is more order in the streets, although a lot of people are running away from town. Adia wanted me to go with him to see his mother who will be at the station seeing her younger son off to Romania tomorrow but I do not want to go. It upsets me too much and I do not sleep. Lenin, a great hero of the people and the revolution arrived at the Finland station today, where huge crowds gathered to cheer and welcome him back to Petrograd from exile where he had been writing books about making the revolution happen.

27TH APRIL 1917 – THURSDAY

Saw Adia in the evening, we went to a cinema and walked home. Lately there is more order in the streets although just now everyone is running away from town. I still do not know if the Sartissons have settled anything about where they are going. Adia wanted me to go with him to see his mother who will be at the station seeing her youngest son off to Roumania. Now he wants to announce that we are 'engaged' to be married!

28TH APRIL 1917 – FRIDAY

I have no news from home. In the evening I went to see Uncle George. They are alright but he looks very ill.

Ida is still unsettled by herself with the children. Pistolkors ran off from Finland where he has been staying to avoid arrest. Ida does not know where she and the children are going to live.

29TH APRIL 1917 – SATURDAY

We are starting to go out again. This evening I went to meet Ida and we went to see the Forrest family. She was very nice, played and sang and we passed a very pleasant two hours with them. We are still waiting to go to our new lodgings. I shall be very glad as all our things are scattered about just now. When we move, I do not know. Ida is quite undecided as to where she is going to live if she manages to get as far as Copenhagen with the three girls.

1ST MAY 1917 – MONDAY

To think that in a few weeks we will all be separated, May, Ida and I. I can't help wondering where on earth we will go to. I believe all the English people are leaving.

3RD MAY 1917 – WEDNESDAY

In the evening, I met Ida and we went into a café and listened to music – met some officers who drove us home and talked a great deal about seeing us again. I hope Adia did not see me as we drove home because there would be such a gigantic row about it if he did.

5TH MAY 1917 – FRIDAY

I went to the dentist at last with Adia. He is still worrying me to be engaged and married before the autumn and I don't know what to say – he is furious because I will not agree.

8TH MAY 1917 – MONDAY

I have been in bed today feeling very ill and weak with a head cold. I have toothache as well. Mrs Kartzev came back from the hospital.

12TH MAY 1917 – FRIDAY

We have been busy all day carrying things to our other house, apartment that is, and I am very tired. I had a letter from Nina Michaelovna who is asking me to go and stay with them. Once again I will have to say no.

13TH MAY 1917 – SATURDAY

We have been carrying things back and forth all day and now as we have no light anywhere I think I will go and see Mrs Forrest.

14TH MAY 1917 – MONDAY

Went to the dentist with Toulia. In the evening I met Ida. We went to a café and talked quietly. She will be going to Sweden with the three girls very soon. Pistolkors is arranging things. They heard Aylia was in Copenhagen. Ida has to get her papers and passport in order now which will be difficult and she is very nervous about taking the children by herself.

17TH MAY 1917 – WEDNESDAY

I have been to the dentist. Only one more visit to go. The bill will come to about 40 roubles.

Letters are now taking about a month on the way. It is very unsettled here. Every day there are processions and the shops are closed today as the shop assistants are on strike for more money. It is very hot today, 21 degrees in the shade!

18TH MAY 1917 – THURSDAY

At 7.00pm Adia rang up to say he has been ill but is going back to the war, a long distance he said. I suppose I will have to see him tomorrow. Ida is going to Smolni tomorrow to see about getting her passport and documents signed. She is very nervous about going there and what questions they will ask. I hope they will not ask her questions about Rasputin and Anna Verubova. She has rehearsed some answers. I think they are bound to ask about Pistolkors. Where is he?

19TH MAY 1917 – FRIDAY

Ida went to the Smolni to have her papers signed. It is the headquarters of the Bolsheviks now. She said there were queues of people everywhere. She was led into a bare, smoke-filled room, after waiting for three hours. The guard at the door shouted, 'Confirm your name,' at her as she entered. There was a desk overflowing with papers, also more in boxes on the floor and telephones ringing everywhere. Ida was shocked to see that it was Lenin sitting behind the desk. We had seen pictures of him in the newspapers when he arrived at the Finland Station. She said he looked quite fierce and her hands were trembling so much that she tried to grip the papers she was carrying very tightly so that he would not see.

'Please sit,' he said, then when she began to speak in Russian she saw the lines on his forehead ease somewhat. 'British subject?' he asked. 'English governess? Give me the name and address of your employers.' She answered exactly as planned, truthfully with no other information added.

'Tell me how it is you speak such good Russian – an English governess – a British subject.'

The same old question we are always asked and we give the same old answer.

'You left here in 1905 and now you wish to run away again – to Sweden?'

She tried to explain that there would be no work for the English governess in future under the new regime. However, of course he was more interested in her employers and the whereabouts of Alexander Pistolkors.

'And these parents who have deserted their children, leaving three small girls without a mother or father, where have they disappeared to?' Ida said she had no information about them.

Ida was well rehearsed in her answers. She said she had no money to keep herself, let alone three children. 'What am I to do with them?' she asked him.

'A very unfortunate situation you find yourself in, Miss Dickinson.'

A long pause followed. 'The mother, Alexandra Taneyeva Pistolkors, the sister of Anna Verubova – you met their aunt frequently I am informed – a constant visitor to Tsarskoe Selo, well known to the guards in fact. Also their grandmother Princess Paley – where are these people who are needed by the children?'

And so the interview went on with probing questions about the Pistolkors family and all their relations. In the end, there was only one solution and that was to take the children to Sweden to be with their mother. She said she had no idea where Pistolkors was and with that her papers were stamped and signed. She had been there about five hours.

Adia did not ring. I have not seen him. I think he has fits of sulking. I am in no fit state to see him and feel very apprehensive about the future. People are saying worse is yet to come. As it is there are very few shops open and to buy anything you have to know a password to get into the shop. Well, at least we have found somewhere to live at last. It is a small very sparsely furnished apartment over some shops which are now closed down on Nadegenskaya street. There are only a few sticks of furniture but at least it is somewhere for Mr Kartzev to stay when he comes out of hospital. All I can think of at the moment is the very dangerous journey Ida is about to undertake with the three children.

20TH MAY 1917 – SATURDAY

May arrived back in town. Ida and I met her and we had time to talk. It was very hot. We discussed going back to England but how to do it we do not know – when we have not enough money to pay for the journey.

21ST MAY 1917 – SUNDAY

The morning we passed in church with the children and in the afternoon we had a service with the priest who came to bless the house we are now living in.

The time is coming nearer for Ida to go away. I wish she did not have to go. Goodness! I cannot think how lonely it will be for me this summer. Adia did not ring.

23RD MAY 1917 – TUESDAY

Adia rang up for me to meet him this evening. We went to see Piotr Petrovitch but he was very busy so we met May and went to the Summer Gardens where we walked and then sat and talked for a while. No news from home.

24TH MAY 1917 – WEDNESDAY

May and I spent the evening with Ida. She is going away next Tuesday morning and has given me her precious photo collection to look after. She is afraid to take it to Sweden as there are several taken in Tsarskoe Selo with Anna Verubova and the Tsarina.

Adia did not ring. Last year at this time we were in Finland but this year we know nothing about whether we will go away or not.

25TH MAY 1917 – THURSDAY

I am quite mad and upset. Everyone is going away. It is very hot in town.

27TH MAY 1917 – SATURDAY

May went back to Finland today – only two more days and Ida will be gone too.

29TH MAY 1917 – MONDAY

Went to say goodbye to Ida in the evening. I felt so sad. Mr and Mrs Forrest also came to say goodbye to her. I left at 11.30 pm, feeling like an orphan.

30TH MAY 1917 – TUESDAY

I have felt lost all day thinking about Ida's long journey to Sweden. She is on her way now. In the evening I went over to her place to collect some books and things that she had left for me in her empty room. I have not seen Adia since last Tuesday. I think he is sulking because I have been spending most of my free time with my sisters. May went on the 27th, so I have said goodbye to both now and I will miss them so much – How awfully lonely I will be this summer.

31ST MAY 1917 – WEDNESDAY

I am sitting at home feeling very lonely. Ida left some money for me to send to mother. I spent the evening reading Chekhov. I think I feel even more dissatisfied with my life than his heroine does even though I am in town because I am not doing anything of any use.

1ST JUNE 1917 – THURSDAY

I went to see my pupil Veronica.

Adia rang and wanted to see me but I stayed at home and wrote letters and read my book. I am in such a bad mood, not wanting to talk to anyone. I feel so lost and lonely – don't want to speak to anyone.

3RD JUNE 1917 – SATURDAY

A very hot day. Stayed at home and wrote letters.

4TH JUNE 1917 – SUNDAY

Pistolkors rang to say that he has not heard from Ida. No more have I! I am very anxious to hear from her. In the evening I went to Mrs Forrest's and we had a drive out to the islands in one of the big cars which was hidden. What an escape! Mr Forrest says that some evening if we set off earlier we will go for a sail. They are a great comfort to me and very sympathetic to our situation, especially for Ida. But even they speak of going away and are undecided about where they will go.

5TH JUNE 1917 – MONDAY

The whole day spent running about sending money off to England and tomorrow I will have to go again. It has gone at a great loss. I had to pay 1,135 roubles for £70; that means it is 160 roubles for £10. In England it is 226; what a great shame it is.

Pistolkors rang to say he has received a telegram from Ida to say she arrived safely in Copenhagen with the children. I spent the evening with the Forrests talking about Ida and how relieved and glad we are that she has arrived in Sweden. Thank God no harm has come to her either from the Germans or the Bolsheviks.

7TH JUNE 1917 – WEDNESDAY

It is stiflingly hot. Now I know what it is like to be in town in the summer and am beginning to long for the country. Before this, we have always been in Finland for the summer even when I was a child. I must write to Ida and ask what has happened to her and ask why she does not write to me.

9TH JUNE 1917 – FRIDAY

Felt very tired all day so am sitting at home. It is very hot. No news from anyone. Trouble is expected in town and we are staying in the house. I wish everything was different. I wish everything would change. I feel pretty bad about everyone going away. We have to queue everywhere now for food and it takes such a long time to get anything with people shouting and jostling and everyone complaining loudly about prices.

11TH JUNE 1917 – SUNDAY

This afternoon I went to visit the Forrests and we all went to the Boat Club. We took a boat out for a row, then had dinner there and then had another row. It was lovely on the river. I wish we were going to some place where there is a river. I would go out rowing every evening and forget all my troubles. May is coming to town for a day on Monday or Tuesday; how nice that will be. We are no nearer to knowing where we are going for the summer. Mrs Kartzev doesn't mention it. Maybe she doesn't want anyone to know.

13TH JUNE 1917 – TUESDAY

We went to the Summer Gardens in the morning and in the afternoon I made some biscuits. This evening I went to see my pupil Veronica. Tomorrow morning I am going to Finland with Mrs Kartzev to see if we can find a villa in Mustamiaki. I suppose May will arrive whilst we are gone.

14TH JUNE 1917 – WEDNESDAY

Early this morning we went off to Finland and of course as I thought, May arrived and we were gone. We are off to the country on Saturday to a villa in Mustamiaki. A sudden decision

which took me by surprise. Mr Kartzev thinks we will be safe –
it will give him time to recover from his gunshot wounds.

15TH JUNE 1917 – THURSDAY

I went to say goodbye to the Forrests because after tomorrow
we are gone from here to Finland, probably until the end of
September maybe October. We talked about Ida and the three
children. Mrs Forrest thinks she was very brave to go on such a
dangerous journey with the children.

16TH JUNE 1917 – FRIDAY

We started to pack at 7.00pm this evening and it is already
2.00am and I am only just going to bed. I have to be up at 5.00am
tomorrow. No news from anyone. I wonder what has happened
to Adia. He went away without saying goodbye. Perhaps he has
gone to France as he said.

19TH JUNE 1917 – MONDAY

It is already Monday but of course I could not write before as we
had no ink. After a lot of hurry and bustle we arrived safely at
this place, Mustamiaki, which is very pretty and we have a lake!
We shall never see anyone or any familiar faces at all. Spent most
of the day unpacking and went to bed early as we have no oil for
the lamps. I slept very badly. We are 8 *versts* from the station so
letters will come very slowly. The food question is very much
complicated. The Finns do not accept Russian money and they
will not change very much either so it is pretty bad.

Tomorrow I am going to bathe in the lake which looks

beautiful especially in the evenings. I go with Big Toulia and when the sun is setting it is exquisite. How lovely everything looks with the fields and quaint little huts in them and the lake with very dark green foliage on the opposite side. I don't know when I have seen anything looking so beautiful. It is so far away from all the chaos of town I could be in another world. We went down to the lake this morning where I undressed behind some bushes and went a long, long way into the lake. The water was about 18 degrees. I could not help forgetting all worries whilst splashing about. After we came out, we lay on the grass and I am turning brown already, also Toulia and Andrei. Our departure was so suddenly decided, I cannot believe I am here in this lovely peaceful place.

Well, Ida does not write a single line to me and Adia is a thing of the past now. I am going to read as much as I can and do some sewing to pass away the time this summer.

20TH JUNE 1917 – TUESDAY

We had quite a big row today. Andrei dropped his watch in the water, then told a complete lie and said he had put it on the sand. He had us searching for three hours until some boys found it in the water and all came to light. I gave him a good, hard smack. He is such a naughty boy and gives me a great deal of trouble.

21ST JUNE 1917 – WEDNESDAY

Mr and Mrs Kartzev went off back to town today and the children and I sat for most of the day in the fields and going for walks. Strange to say, I have not felt hot once here. I must say Mustamiaki is a beautiful place to spend the summer and especially if you had some nice friends with you. I wish…

22ND JUNE 1917 – THURSDAY

A day passed as usual. We have been lying in the fields and bathing in the lake. It is very quiet here, almost like being in another world.

Still no letters from anyone. I am quite sunburnt now. I have started sewing some little serviettes. I should love to have a letter from home.

23RD JUNE 1917 – FRIDAY

We are going to have a bonfire in the woods tonight as it is a big holiday here. We shall roast some potatoes and I will think of my childhood days when we were all together and when the Finns used to have huge bonfires on the sands. They used to dress up in bright colours and dance but now they do not celebrate the 23rd June so much. Yesterday Mrs Kartzev brought me a letter from Nina Michaelovna and a postcard from May.

The day passed very slowly, walking about. I have just put the children to bed and am going off to the wood to light the fire. I am getting quite anxious about not having any letters from mother or Ida. I can't help wondering what has happened to her in Stockholm or has she gone on to Copenhagen? Who will be dressing Aylia's hair and massaging her and doing her nails – It will be really hard to break away from Aylia and the children, if she continues the routine she had here.

24TH JUNE 1917 – SATURDAY

Rain has been falling since midday. We had a walk in the morning and now it is 8.00pm and I have just finished with the children. The sun has just come out for the first time today. I have been sewing and making English biscuits and when Mrs Kartzev returns from the shop I am going for a walk. It will be damp but the perfume after the rain will be wonderful.

It is just a week since we arrived here and I have heard nothing from Ida. Tomorrow, Sunday, we are going to the church which is a very long walk away. Everything is so quiet here, the Revolution seems so far off and a thing of the past. We have no idea what is happening in Petrograd.

I am very glad I have kept up with this diary. It may be of interest to read in the future, wherever I am. I wish I could look into the future. How will my free time be spent next year?

25TH JUNE 1917 – SUNDAY

A dark and dreary day, raining most of the time. Cleared up near 7.00pm. Nothing happened and am afraid I will grow very fat here as I drink so much milk. No news from anyone. I am just going out for a walk before tea and then it is bedtime again. We still have no lamp oil and so I cannot read.

26TH JUNE 1917 – MONDAY

We all went for a long walk this morning. I keep deciding to get up early but have not been up before 7.30am. Lay in the grass and then went to buy vegetables. Tea, dinner, and there is the whole day gone, so very monotonous, again. The children are happy and carefree and make me smile but one cannot forget what is happening in Petrograd.

27TH JUNE 1917 - TUESDAY

Very hot today. Went for a long walk in the morning and we lay in the fields until tea. After that, I went to the post with some letters and then helped to prepare dinner. Had some games with the children and have just finished putting them to bed. Perhaps I will walk down to the lake. No news from anyone. I wonder what Ida is thinking, not to write.

28TH JUNE 1917 - WEDNESDAY

Walked to the station and back – the railwaymen are on strike – I hope not for long as I cannot get even one letter and that is so dreary. I long to get a letter from mother and to hear about what is happening to them in England.

29TH JUNE 1917 - THURSDAY

It was a lovely morning so we bathed in the lake and the day passed as usual. No news. The railwaymen are still on strike. This evening I planted some radish seeds and it took all evening. I am doing very little reading.

30TH JUNE 1917 - FRIDAY

It was very hot today. The day has passed in the most monotonous way – eating, walking and the children playing. The trains have started to run again I think, so I may just get a letter in the course of a day or so. I have to take water to the wash-house now. How slowly the time is passing. Last summer it was so much jollier with more people and dancing (my favourite pastime), tennis and all that. Here it is so very lonely. As for Adia, I do not know what has happened to him. No news from home. The Revolution has changed everything. Ida is gone, May I cannot see. Oh, dear! How much I like to grumble. Perhaps worse times will come and then I will be glad to remember this particular time and wish it all back again. I hardly think so now. I have only the scenery and the beauty of this place to remember of this summer.

1ST JULY 1917 – SATURDAY

Quite out of temper. No news from anyone. Sent postcards to all my aunts in England and wrote to Pistolkors asking about Ida. It is a beautiful evening but I am too tired to move so will sit in my room.

Mr Kartzev fainted this morning and had to be carried to bed where he stayed all day.

2ND JULY 1917 – SUNDAY

Well, we have been here more than two weeks! Nothing special has happened. Bathed in the lake and had a walk. No news from anyone. We had strawberries for the first time today, paying one rouble for a pound. Provisions are very dear: eggs 2R. 30k for 10, meat 2 roubles, milk 85 kopeks a bottle. I wonder if it will ever be cheaper again. The time has been changed in Petrograd and we are keeping it up here and go to bed at 9.00pm and get up at 7.00am, or earlier. The children will have to get used to it.

Mr Kartzev still in bed. I have to keep the children very quiet. It is not easy.

3RD JULY 1917 – MONDAY

Sent off a letter to Nina Michaelovna. Sat in the hay which has just been cut down. Bathed in the morning. It is the most beautiful evening but I am sitting in the house, reading. No letters from anyone. I am so anxious to hear about my sisters.

4TH JULY 1917 – TUESDAY

We have been looking for mushrooms. We hear there is great trouble again in Petrograd. Some of the regiments do not want to go to the war but the sailors from Kronstadt have arrived with their cannons and there is a lot of shooting going on all over the place. Today it is written that there was shooting in our street, Nadegenskaya. I wonder if our house will be plundered again. I suppose it is a good thing that we are in Finland. I am writing a letter to mother again.

5TH JULY 1917 – WEDNESDAY

No news. Rained all day. Went bathing in the lake after tea, the most pleasant occupation of the whole day. It is the most beautiful evening but when you have no one to go out with it is so lonely.

6TH JULY 1917 – THURSDAY

At last, a letter from May inviting me to go and visit her at Sartisson's villa in Terijoki. It will be a kind of escape from my daily routine here. I will be able to see some different people so I think I might go for a few days if I can get away.

7TH JULY 1917 – FRIDAY

All the fields look very bare now that the hay is gathered in. Spent the day walking about, mostly looking for provisions.

Tomorrow we will have been here for three weeks. I wonder why Mrs Forrest doesn't write to me – well, I suppose I am forgotten when out of sight and she has a lot of friends in Petrograd.

8TH JULY 1917 – SATURDAY

Went gathering mushrooms and berries and fried the mushrooms for lunch. We have no servant now. We went to bathe, returned for tea and made some biscuits and cleaned all the berries for dinner. After a few more household duties, putting the children to bed and watering the radishes and vegetables, it's already 8.30pm. The minister Grigorovitch is here so he, big Toulia and I are going to walk around the lake. I would dearly love to have a letter from England but suppose that is impossible as there is great disorder in Petrograd. The shooting is continuing and now they say that some of the army from the front are being brought back to put the town in order. The workmen are not working and it is reported that there is chaos everywhere.

9TH JULY 1917 – SUNDAY

I am going to May in Terijoki tomorrow! Wonder of wonders! I received a letter from Alexander Pistolkors, in which he says that Ida is very upset, too much upset to write and that she wants to go from Sweden to England. Like me, she has had enough of all the chaos but parting with the children will be hard. It is rumoured that the Tsarina, Tsar and family are to be exiled to the Crimea. They are still under arrest at Tsarskoe Selo. Anna Verubova has been imprisoned in the Peter and Paul Fortress, to be exact in the grim Troubetskoy prison dungeons. The Bolsheviks have dug graves for the people who died for the Revolution in Tsarskoe Selo, right in front of the Alexander Palace in full view of the windows. Hatred for the Tsar has grown to such a pitch amongst the masses of the people that they have sworn to kill every member of the Romanov family and are marching about shouting, 'Death to the Romanovs,' not just, 'Down with the Tsar.' Where has all this hatred suddenly come from? People are starving and thousands are being killed in the war. I expect Ida feels even lonelier than I do. The children have been reunited with their mother in Copenhagen, so that is one good thing. It is 4 years now since Germany declared war on us.

10TH JULY 1917 MONDAY

Got up very early. Mrs Kartzev and Toulia accompanied me to Terijoki where I left them and went on to stay with May at the Sartissons. Spent the day there very quietly. Nothing has changed in their life and I could imagine myself back in last September when I was here at their house. Vava has grown taller and a very talkative little girl she is. Her English is good, thanks to May who speaks English to her all the time.

11TH JULY 1917 – TUESDAY

Last night we had a bonfire also went out rowing in a boat on the sea. It was very shallow. May and I talked non stop until midnight, about Ida and home. May had a letter from mother but it is a very old one.

12TH JULY 1917 - WEDNESDAY

Mrs Sartisson asked me to bake some bread which I rather like doing – in the evening, May said I would dance for them. All the relations gathered round and I did one or two dances but how heavy on my feet I have got being without practice! I go back to Mustamiaki on the 14th July. Mr Sartisson is not here; he is now without a job and is looking for another position somewhere in Europe. They do not think the revolution will reach here and Mrs Sartisson carries on just as before since they are more or less self sufficient with plenty of eggs and milk – very fortunate.

15TH JULY 1917 - SATURDAY

Got up to the old life again this morning and first of all baked 9lbs of flour. A letter from Adia arrived. I thought he had forgotten my existence after all this time – it was written on 14th June. After lunch we went in a boat rowing on the lake and picked some lilies out of the water.

17TH JULY 1917 - SATURDAY

A long day in Vyborg shopping – bought some shoes which cost 60 marks – that is about 57 roubles. I suppose I should be saving money but was desperately in need of them. There's no point in saving money now as we will never have enough to pay for the journey home – another letter from Adia when I got back which he had managed to get someone to write in English – I wonder why? I will reply in English.

23RD JULY 1917 – SUNDAY

Another ordinary day spent as usual. Sometimes, sitting down to write my diary, I am in despair because one day is so much like another. There is very little to write about – Mr Kartzev says provisions are very hard to get in Petrograd and that we will stay here for as long as possible. He is even more nervous now since the naval college was occupied – How many more weeks of this monotonous, tedious life will I have to endure? Sometimes think I may run away like Ida did from the Souvorins – but have nowhere to run to.

27TH JULY 1917 – THURSDAY

The post is taking such a long time these days, at least two weeks. A very sad day for the children as our little dog 'Moorman' was killed by another dog and we had to bury him in the woods.

29TH JULY 1917 – SATURDAY

Just fancy I am 24 years old today. I am quite the old maid governess now. It is now 8.00pm and the children are going to bed. Wish I could just float through the sky over to England and talk to my mother. I remember she was always such a great fan of royalty. She knew all the royalty connections in Europe – all Queen Victoria's children, their marriages and their children. I wonder what she thinks – or if she even knows about the Tsar and his family. Her favourite one was the Grand Duchess Ella, the Tsarina's sister, after whom our own youngest sister was named. No doubt she is glad that she made the decision to leave Russia in 1905, even though my father did not want to go. No news from anyone – no birthday cards or letters – I suppose I shall go to bed and read.

30TH JULY 1917 – SUNDAY

I wonder how long it will take for a letter to come from Adia – Ivan Grigorovitch is going to town on the 9th of August, so he will forward letters if there are any there. He has promised to paint a small oil picture for me.

3RD AUGUST 1917 – THURSDAY

Since my birthday came and went with no card from mother I am remembering so much from past birthdays – how she would spoil me with cakes and presents. Whenever she went out on a visit she would always bring back some kind of curious, little toy for each of us. I remember her once going on a trip to Moscow when Father took her to stay with friends there to see the Coronation celebrations.

It was much discussed and described in every detail for years afterwards because during the festivities a great tragedy took place. Enormous crowds gathered to see the procession and the golden coaches carrying the Tsar, Tsarina and the Dowager Empress. Souvenir coronation cups were to be given away and our mother had set her heart on having one of these. People began to gather, some even spent the night at the Khodinka field, a big field on the outskirts of town where there was a fair and merry-go-rounds, stalls and puppet shows. A pavilion, a model of the Petrovskoe Palace, was built there for the Tsar and Tsarina, where they could stand on a balcony to acknowledge the crowds and this was where the coronation cups were to be given away.

Our father told us how he had jostled through the crowds and managed to get one of these cups which were enamelled with the double headed eagle and the date 1896 on the side. Fortunately they had arrived early and left as soon as they were able to get away from the huge crowds. They were very lucky to make their escape as not much later a whole mass of people converged from all sides of the field and rushed into a terrible stampede where many were suffocated and trampled to death. They said that over 1,400 people died that day in the stampede to get the cups. After that our mother was always afraid of crowds and passed on her fear to all of us. The coronation cup was never used but remained with mother's collection of china and was transported back to Oldham.

Have been on two long walks, one was to get provisions, and another to try to get butter. It is awfully dear. No news from anyone. Mrs Kartzev is going to Vyborg tomorrow to get provisions.

4TH AUGUST 1917 – FRIDAY

I have felt tired and depressed today. Mrs Kartzev and her sister Toulia are away in Vyborg and will return about 9.00pm. I have sent so many cards and letters and somehow you begin to lose hope when there is no answer. Wish Ida would write as I can't help wondering what has happened to her. I wonder if we should go back to England where perhaps we could find some kind of work in Manchester.

Everything is so quiet here when Mrs Kartzev and Toulia are away. She, Mrs K that is, does talk quite a lot sometimes but nothing like as much as Nina Michaelovna. I felt much more at home with the Loukin family than I do here.

They say the food question is very bad in Petrograd and getting worse every day, with prices rising all the time.

5TH AUGUST 1917 – SATURDAY

Still hot. It is already dark and it is only 9.00pm. I have written another letter to May, also one to my brother Leslie and one to mother. No letters for me. Everyone has forgotten me.

We went to try to get flour but could not get any. I bathed twice today. The water was quite warm. We have walked about a good deal today.

6TH AUGUST 1917 – SUNDAY

As I returned from church with the children Mrs Kartzev was waiting at the door and said, 'You have a visitor – Adia!' What a great surprise that was. His right arm was in a sling but he stood up, smiling as usual and kissed me on both cheeks. He is now very thin and seems to look much more serious – in fact older.

After lunch Mrs Kartzev said I was free for the rest of the day. She made such a fuss of him – offering him the most comfortable chairs and plying him with tea and cakes. We went for a walk around the lake; he has a bullet wound in his arm but fortunately it hasn't touched the bone.

'How peaceful it is here!' – He had to keep on repeating this. I suppose such a change from Petrograd and the horrors of the trenches – We talked about last summer in Knokkola and the happy times we spent there but it was not long before he was asking about when we were to be married and how he was going to leave the army. He dreams of a new life with me somewhere away from all the mayhem in Petrograd. He is not very practical and refuses to see how impossible it would be, however much I tell him it is so. 'If you are so unhappy here, why not run away if you really want to? Come back to Petrograd with me and we will find somewhere for you to live. Come back to Petrograd on the next train with me,' he said. I was silent, said nothing for a long time – how could I run away, though the temptation to do just that was very great. Common sense tells me it would all end in disaster. He will be going back to the war again very soon – he is staying overnight and will catch the train back tomorrow.

Mrs Kartzev said he could stay with us as long as he wanted but he has to go back tomorrow – to the hospital in Petrograd. I think he just escaped from there and told no one where he was going, so he will have to face the music when he gets back. No doubt he will be in great trouble for going missing and have to face a court martial or something equivalent.

7TH AUGUST 1917 – MONDAY

Up very early as I am to accompany him to the station. He bid his farewells to the Kartzevs and children and we set off for the station – rather a long walk – at about 10.00am. Last night I decided to go back to Petrograd with him so stuffed a few things into his bag and carried just bare necessities in my own. Said not a word to the Kartzevs – felt awful about doing this but nevertheless jumped on the train to Petrograd with him. On reaching town he asked me to wait in a café for an hour or so – where I had a glass of tea – while he reported in at the hospital and found somewhere for me to stay. I sat watching all the people pass by, a lot of them leaving town with heavy suitcases. Most looked badly dressed and desperate – there is hardly any food in the shops and a lot of people are starving. After an hour had passed I knew I could not do this awful thing. What would my sister May have to say about it? How selfish she would think I was. Mrs Kartzev would be so worried about what had happened to me and the children would be crying – and what would mother and father think of me?

The next train back to Finland, stopping at Mustamiaki, was due – I could sit there waiting no longer. All at once I jumped up, ran for the train and was on my way back just before his return was due.

8TH AUGUST 1917 – TUESDAY

Have spent tonight writing to Adia. I apologised to Mrs Kartzev for being so late getting back from the station and all is returned to normal as if nothing had happened.

9TH AUGUST 1917 – WEDNESDAY

When we were going to the shoemaker's, we saw two carts filled with black coffins go flying past followed by about thirty more going at such speed. The carts were on their way to funerals. Some people were crying as they raced past us, all covered in dust so that they seemed to be all dressed in grey. It was very strange to see the clouds of dust rising up. It was so funny. It looked like a racing competition the rate they were going with the horses. How awful of me, I couldn't help laughing it was so strange, and where were they taking the bodies to be buried? A very strange sight indeed. Were these people who had died in the revolution I wonder – and where were their bodies going to be buried in such a great hurry.

10TH AUGUST 1917 – THURSDAY

We went to gather whimberries and came back with 6 pounds altogether. I am anxiously waiting for a letter from England and to know about Ida. She was not eating anything very much when she left because she was anticipating the awful journey and could not sleep. Some people escape by crossing the Baltic to Stockholm, paying huge sums of money to bribe the sailors to take them over the partly frozen sea on sledges in the winter; some of them make it to the other side but they take a great risk because sometimes the sailors will take their money and disappear without trace. I wonder if Adia thinks we could escape in this way.

12TH AUGUST 1917 – SATURDAY

Got up very early and went for a walk. Baked with some brown flour we managed to buy. We tried to catch fish in the lake this afternoon but had no luck.

13TH AUGUST 1917 – SUNDAY

Mrs Kartzev and her father arrived back with a postcard from mother, dated 2nd July. They are all well and will send me a letter very soon. Must remember to send card to Natasha. It is her birthday on the 26th and the post will take a long time to travel.

15TH AUGUST 1917 – TUESDAY

Today received a letter from Adia. He is very lonely and says he will return in September or October. We got up at 5.00am and went to gather whimberries. On the way we killed a snake and the children got quite excited about it. They are speaking English pretty well now and somehow even manage to quarrel in English. Mrs Kartzev and her father have gone back to town.

17TH AUGUST 1917 – THURSDAY

It has been raining all day. I had a letter from my old pupil, Veronica. Her father is now a very highly decorated general in command of an army. Have sent letters to May and Natasha and must write to Adia tonight.

18TH AUGUST 1917 – FRIDAY

We had to go a very long way today to buy vegetables and only got home at 2.00pm. After tea we went for a bathe in the lake.

19TH AUGUST 1917 – SATURDAY

Just before lunch Mrs Kartzev and her father arrived back from town but I did not receive any letters from England.

20TH AUGUST 1917 – SUNDAY

We all went for a very long walk to the station and the church nearby where we went to the service. We were late back for lunch. No news from anyone. Feel very sad to have no letters after I have written so many.

22ND AUGUST 1917 – TUESDAY

The whole day rain was coming down. Went into the wood looking for white mushrooms. No news.

23RD AUGUST 1917 – WEDNESDAY

This morning we went to Terijoki to buy a jacket for big Toulia. It was raining on and off all day. Coming home we had a good laugh with the cabman which I encouraged for the sake of a joke.

Still no news. I am sitting at my little table with the smelly oil lamp and everything is quiet. They have all gone to bed.

I am beginning to think seriously about going to England. May says she will go back to England if Mrs Sartisson decides to go to Mr Sartisson who is now in a very dreary place in Nijni but if they are staying in Finland she will stop here. So that question is still in the air.

It would be horrid for me to go and leave Adia but on the other hand do not feel like being married to him. He is such a boy – too young. Then money matters are so complicated nowadays. You cannot marry without money as everything is tremendously dear. I will have to trust in God, and trust he will arrange my fate somehow but cannot see any solution to my problems. Life here is so isolated and utterly boring – it is almost like being imprisoned. Adia says the Tsar, Tsarina and the whole family have been taken from the Alexander Palace and put on a train to Siberia – it is now occupied by the Red Guards.

24TH AUGUST 1917 – THURSDAY

A whole day of rain. Went to find mushrooms. Mrs Kartzev has gone to Vyborg to buy provisions. We have heard that the Cossacks are coming to stay in our village. I do not know what we will do then as they will probably grab all the food.

25TH AUGUST 1917 – FRIDAY

Mrs Kartzev returned yesterday evening, much upset because she had forgotten her passport in Vyborg. This morning she and I set off on foot for the long walk to the station. I did not feel very well the whole day.

26TH AUGUST 1917 – SATURDAY

It is the Names Day today of both Toulias. I was in bed the whole day. My temperature was very high, over 40 degrees – must have caught a bad cold.

27TH AUGUST 1917 – SUNDAY

Feel very weak. Only got out of bed for an hour. For the first time for three or four days the sun is shining. They have all gone to church so it is very quiet in the house. I wonder if I have a letter in town from England or from Ida. I expect that Aylia will not want her to return to England but at this moment we do not know for sure where she is. I do not think Ida will want to stay in Copenhagen.

28TH AUGUST 1917 – MONDAY

Just waiting for letters from everyone. It rained the whole night and I had terrible nightmares. Not much sleep. Tomorrow may be able to go out for a walk. The children are making a terrible row.

29TH AUGUST 1917 – TUESDAY

Went out for a little walk in the woods and found some white mushrooms. The newspaper reports that things are very bad in Petrograd. There is expected to be a big battle between the new government and General Kornilov who wants to take over the parliament and replace Kerenski. He has over 70,000 men and aims to cut off Petrograd so that no food will come in. Perhaps it is a good thing that we are in Finland.

Had a letter from May. Now she says she wants to go to Nijni and is coming to see me tomorrow.

30TH AUGUST 1917 – WEDNESDAY

I was surprised to see May. She arrived with a letter from Mrs Sartisson who proposes that I go to Nijni with them. She says I can live with them and give lessons, or get another post there. It was so sudden! May only stayed for an hour and I feel quite dazed. Of course would like to be with May but Nijni Novgorod? Mrs Kartzev is now going mad, saying I must not go on any account and that she cannot manage without me. Tonight, I shall go dotty as well, I think.

31ST AUGUST 1917 – THURSDAY

Mrs Kartzev keeps talking to me all the time and begging me not to leave them. I half promised May that I would go with her but what if I find myself with another job I do not like and what if we have to move again? How silly it is that I cannot make a definite decision for myself. How much longer can the war go on? When will it end?

1ST SEPTEMBER 1917 – FRIDAY

It is such a temptation to run off to Nijni with May. Still do not know what to do and Mrs Kartzev is very upset and so are the children and big Toulia, all asking me not to leave them. I am waiting impatiently for a letter from May now.

2ND SEPTEMBER 1917 – SATURDAY

A day of great impatience and disappointment, no letter from May. Mrs Kartzev has set her mind on me staying with them.

Here it is terribly dull just now, the weather is much colder and there is nothing to do in the house. I have had awful dreams these last few nights, no doubt because I am so unsettled about the future.

3RD SEPTEMBER 1917 – SUNDAY

Russian money keeps dropping in value so we may not be able to stop here much longer. In Vyborg the soldiers killed some officers and in Petrograd the disorder is so terrible that it will be impossible to live there this winter.

I have read all my books and have nothing left. We found a lot of mushrooms today. We are going to dry them. It is just 9.00pm and am sitting down to drink tea. No word from May about going to Nijni.

4TH SEPTEMBER 1917 – MONDAY

Managed to buy some more flour. Dull and rainy day. Was so anxious to hear from May and received a postcard today. It seems they are not going just yet and they don't know when they will leave for Nijni. I feel very cross about it all. Mrs Kartzev says we are going back to town on the 7th September, that is on Thursday so we are already packing up.

17TH SEPTEMBER 1917 – SUNDAY

I have not written a word for such a long time. May gave me another fright by saying she was going but they have not gone yet. Everything is so uncertain.

We did not stay in town very long. Mrs Kartzev says we are here until the end of the month. I now want to change my passport and wonder if they will give me my old Russian one. We are going to town tomorrow for 2 days, taking some things back to our apartment on Nadegenskaya. I sold my summer coat for 60 roubles when we went back last time. It seems clothes are now more valuable than money these days.

19TH SEPTEMBER 1917 – TUESDAY

There were no letters for me in town. We did a great deal of running about collecting things from various places where they had been stored. Phoned May as soon as I got here. She is staying in Finland until the end of this month.

20TH SEPTEMBER 1917 – WEDNESDAY

Rainy day. Mr Kartzev mended a pair of low shoes for me. He is repairing all our shoes with India rubber soles as we can't afford to buy any now because they are such a high price. No news of any sort. It is so dark, dull and rainy. I shall be glad to go back to town now.

23RD SEPTEMBER 1917 – SATURDAY

Very glad today is over; it has been very long, dull and

monotonous. Mrs Kartzev and her father arrived back from town after lunch and it is now decided that we will leave here on the 1st October. They brought no letters. These dark, grey autumn days are so melancholy, the ground is covered with dead leaves and the mushrooms are gone. People are leaving Mustamiaki now as it is lonely and cold in the evenings.

The troubles in town have not stopped and many have left to live elsewhere. Food, they say, is very difficult to get and very expensive. I still do not know whether I shall leave or not. I do not know how the poor people manage to live.

24TH SEPTEMBER 1917 – SUNDAY

I was ill all night long and lay in bed the whole day with terrible pains in my stomach and head. Postcard from May – she is coming to town on the 2nd October – not very far off.

26TH SEPTEMBER 1917 – TUESDAY

The sun shone all day so felt better but have been sleeping very badly and hope I am not going back to my nights of insomnia. Mr Grigorovitch went back to town today, for good. The day passed very slowly. This evening had a letter from home and everything is quite alright with them. Will be so glad to go back to town as it is quite cold here now. Made bread and vegetable pies today – seem to have turned into the chief cook here and they are very glad of my bread-making skills. Everything is so tremendously expensive now, and that is if you can get it.

30TH SEPTEMBER 1917 – SATURDAY

Arrived back in town safely and spent the day unpacking. It is rather dull in town now. The lanterns are all painted green, yellow and red and look very gloomy. Received newspapers from England. Rules are changed in the hour, everything is so mixed up.

3RD OCTOBER 1917 – TUESDAY

This evening went out to see May. Mrs Sartisson has sent some very nice material to make a skirt. We had a good chat about things but are no nearer deciding what to do. Many places of business are closing. Probably we shall be here until the Spring. Everyone is selling things at the Jews' market. I have been to Loukin's for a coat I left there which I can sell.

10TH OCTOBER 1917 – TUESDAY

Have been going out a lot lately and had no time for my diary. May and I have been to Mrs Forrest's. She is holding musical evenings where she plays and sings and other musicians join her. It is a real delight to see other people and listen to the music after being isolated for so long in Mustamiaki. I was almost tempted to get up and dance for them.

11TH OCTOBER 1917 – WEDNESDAY

Sold my coat for 110 roubles. I am very glad as I bought it for 100 roubles and wore it for the whole of one winter. May was also selling things. We might get enough money to pay the fare back to England. It is true that we are getting good wages but it is all worth nothing at this rate of exchange and I have nothing to send home to mother. Clothes are now more valuable than money. People are selling even old, patched underclothes and suits fetch fabulous prices. May says the food question is just as bad in all the towns which is why they decided not to go to Nijni. The trams are awfully crowded with soldiers who do not pay anything and occupy all the seats. May's place, the Sartisson's apartment in Petrograd, is only about 20 minutes away, so I shall walk. The fares are increased to 15 roubles, so that to travel long distances is a great hardship. An *izvoschik* (horse drawn cab) will not go the length of a few houses now for less than three roubles; five, ten or fifteen roubles are quite ordinary fares.

We are considered to be in a war zone and have alarms in case of Zeppelin raids but don't think they will come once the frost sets in. Everything now depends on the army and no one seems to know how things will turn out. A great part of the Russian army is going to be disbanded, all those aged 43 and over. Mr Sartisson is 43 but we do not know whether this concerns officers. May says it would be easier to leave Mrs Sartisson if he came home, as she does not want to leave her alone.

12TH OCTOBER 1917 - THURSDAY

I am framing two small watercolours which Mr Grigorovitch gave me when we were in Mustamiaki. May rang to say Ida is back in England. She must have received a letter – such a relief to know she is safely back with our mother and father. I am making a skirt with the material Mrs Sartisson gave me. It will only cost 28 roubles.

14TH OCTOBER 1917 – SATURDAY

We went to have tea at Mrs Forrest's. They are much the same and their son Shura has grown a lot whilst I've been away. We went to a dance in the evening. It was very nice, the music was good and I danced a lot and quite forgot about all my worries for a while.

16TH OCTOBER 1917 – MONDAY

I have been over to the Forrests' again. It was a very noisy evening, everyone talking about the war. There were two officers and another gentleman there who say the British Consul may help to pay our fares back to England. Can that be true?

20TH OCTOBER 1917 – FRIDAY

They were expecting more trouble in the streets but it didn't come off. Everything stayed quiet. The children are being remarkably good, although they do not understand what is going on, they seem to know how dangerous our situation is.

21ST OCTOBER 1917 – SATURDAY

Got a terrible cold so stayed in all day. Tomorrow the tailor is coming to measure my skirt.

23RD OCTOBER 1917 – MONDAY

Another day at home as my cold is no better. An awful day, there is no electricity. I am going out with Mrs Forrest tomorrow to sell some clothes and try to get some money together.

24TH OCTOBER 1917 – TUESDAY

My cold is no better so stayed indoors. All the bridges are up and the sailors from Kronstadt have arrived and are on guard. They say Kerenski is in great danger.

25TH OCTOBER 1917 – WEDNESDAY

Feeling better so have been out today. We saw some officers arrested by sailors. The Winter Palace is surrounded so it looks as though Kerenski's reign is finished.

11.30pm – Not going to bed at all tonight as there is shooting all over the place. The Winter Palace is being bombarded. Some say that there will be a new government tonight, others say that Nicholas will be back on the throne. I don't see how that can happen. Mrs Kartzev has just told me to dress the children in case we have to run like we did on February 27th. No one here can be certain of surviving the night. I wonder if there will be anything left of the Palace in the morning.

Bands of sailors are going about shooting the Jews and other soldiers are robbing all the houses; some companies are shouting, 'Down with the Capitalists,' and there is just absolute chaos outside. It may seem strange to write in such a cool hand about it all but what on earth can one do? Our servants, the ones who stayed with us, are all frightened to death and praying at the icon every minute. I can hear shooting on the Litaeney and that is very near. I suppose I had better dress the children as Mrs Kartzev is getting so nervous and excited about it all again. I will spend the night writing letters.

26TH OCTOBER 1917 – THURSDAY

The Palace and all the post offices and government buildings were taken by the Bolsheviks. None of the newspapers are allowed to be printed, except the ones the Bolsheviks control. Kerenski left the Palace and it is said that he is off to the front to recruit soldiers to come over to his side. Then there will be a big fight. The streets round about us are pretty quiet just now but all through the night the shooting went on near the Winter Palace and on the Morskaya. What a good thing that Ida is not there.

27TH OCTOBER 1917 – FRIDAY

A new government is proclaimed today. Everything seems to be in such a muddle and no one actually knows what is happening. Kerenski is coming to the city with an army of soldiers. We have heard that the English are not far off, in fact at Archangel and the Japanese in Vladivostok.

Nina Michaelovna has arrived back in town so I will go to see her tomorrow, also Mrs Forrest has invited me to lunch. I will be glad to go out. We have been in the house all day long. Both children have a cold. I have been sewing a small tablecloth in the evenings. No news from England. I wish I was going there more than ever now. Mrs Kartzev is asleep on the window sill. No one is undressing at night. I hate sleeping in my clothes. The sailors are grabbing everything they can get out of the Palace.

28TH OCTOBER 1917 – SATURDAY

A rather exciting day considering my routine. Have been to see Nina Michaelovna. She wants me to go and live with them in the South – she suggests that both May and I could go. I don't think May will leave the Sartissons.

Kerenski is two *versts* from town and a big fight is expected. Soldiers are stopping all motorcars at the bridges so the streets are pretty quiet.

I think Adia must be dead. He has not written to me for a very long time.

One day next week I will take May to see Nina Michaelovna. I like her because somehow you can feel at home there with her. Natasha and Petya still cry when they remember me. Our lights go out at midnight or earlier and so now I will stop.

29TH OCTOBER 1917 – SUNDAY

A very dull day indoors. No news from England. Kerenski's men have surrounded the city. There was some very heavy fighting – about a hundred *Junkers* against 5,500 Bolsheviks. Of course, all the hundred were killed. The Morskaya, where Ida lived is in a terrible state.

All the houses are locked up at 9.00pm. They say the town is in martial readiness, whatever that means. I feel sick to death of it all and just want to get away somewhere. I wonder when Kerenski will enter the city and what will happen. People are saying that those in power in the government, including Kerenski, are all cheats and liars. Mr and Mrs Forrest are thinking of going to England.

30TH OCTOBER 1917 – MONDAY

Still no news of Kerenski's movements or whereabouts. The telephones are cut off altogether so cannot phone anyone. Shooting again in the Litaeney near to the Forrests and even on their gate. No food is coming into the town now and only one station is open and no newspapers on sale at all.

I went to see Mrs Forrest in the afternoon and found her very upset about everything, mainly about the Bolsheviks looting the houses. Mr Kartzev takes his turn in standing on duty with a revolver in front of our house. Mrs Kartzev has just been in and asked if I was going to England and when I would go. Of course I had no answer for her.

31ST OCTOBER 1917 – TUESDAY

None of the ministries are working and all are on strike. The famous Red Guards, as the workmen are called, go about killing and robbing the houses. The Germans are quite near but no one seems to care very much. This evening shooting started up yet again at the corner of our street. The servant ran in panic-stricken about the lights being on and said they must all be put out at once as the soldiers were shooting at the windows.

1ST NOVEMBER 1917 – WEDNESDAY

May arrived this morning and we had quite a serious discussion about going back to England. She brought a letter at last from Ida who has decided to stay in England, in spite of desperate pleas from Pistolkors for her to go back to Copenhagen. Aylia is very much enamoured by the Russian ambassador there. The three little girls cry for Ida to come back.

The town is still under siege but Kerenski is retreating. The telephone is working again but one is only allowed to speak about war business.

May is going back to Finland tonight as it is so bad here in town with no food coming in and all the shooting going on. We, that is to say the Kartzevs, are going to stick it out.

2ND NOVEMBER 1917 – THURSDAY

Another dull day spent indoors. Mrs Kartzev is afraid to go out or let the children out. The latest report is that Kerenski is not moving. I tried to speak to the Forrests by telephone but the soldiers do not know how to answer.

3RD NOVEMBER 1917 – FRIDAY

Another long day. The Bolsheviks seem to be winning the battle. Kerenski is said to have shot himself but I don't know if that is true. I am going to telephone to Adia's mother's house to find out what has happened to him.

The Finnish railway is on strike so May cannot return. I am sick and tired of staying here and want very much to get to England somehow, even though I know I have not enough money for the journey. I will go to the passport office tomorrow.

4TH NOVEMBER 1917 – SATURDAY

Big Toulia is sitting here with me and we are both very tired.

MISS DAISY IS THE PERSON I LOVE BEST AFTER MY FATHER. SHE IS SUCH A DARLING. I WILL MISS HER VERY MUCH WHEN SHE IS GONE. DAISY LIKES TO EAT EGGS. TOULIA LIKES TO DRAW EGGS. This is little Toulia's entry in my diary. No news at all from anyone.

5TH NOVEMBER 1917 SUNDAY

Went out for half an hour as everything has quietened down. Kerenski is somewhere but no one knows where. The shooting has finished and now the Bolsheviks are in power. There are dreadful rumours going around about awful cruelties and many deaths. The newspapers have been an absolute puzzle to read as what is written in one is flatly denied in another. May says the peasants are gathering moss in Finland to make black bread.

I am going to the British Consulate, if it is still there, to ask how I can get to England as I have not enough money to take me. Anyway, Russian money is not accepted I have heard. Snow fell today and it looks very wintry and bleak.

6TH NOVEMBER 1917 – MONDAY

Went to the Consulate and got a form to fill in. Yes, I actually got a form to fill in! Before I knew it, I had quite decided to go to England. It will be dreadfully dear but I do not want to be on my own this winter, wasting my time and my life like I have done all this past summer. I am going to write to May to this effect, otherwise she will never move. It may be worse in the way of business in England but we will be with the family or at least have a family. Adia must have forgotten all about me. He is still alive somewhere, according to his mother. I wonder what he will think when he knows I am going away.

7TH NOVEMBER 1917 – TUESDAY

Trouble expected again. Kartzevs now thinking of going to Finland again. I certainly do not want to go there. All the different political parties are going head-to-head with each other. Went to see the Forrests and there I saw a man who is going back to England tomorrow and he said he had an awful time trying to get his papers signed. I wish I had gone long ago.

8TH NOVEMBER 1917 – WEDNESDAY

Went to see Nina Michaelovna. She is going to Moscow to look for her brother who is in hospital there and then she will go South to Tiflis. She wants me to go with them very much now.

I have heard that Adia is married but do not know if it is true. I can go to England with a clear conscience if it is true. This is a rumour from Shoulkovski, a great joker so doubt whether this is true.

The Bolsheviks have taken the government bank and used thousands of roubles to pay their Red Guards, sailors, soldiers etc. The trains are running to Finland and do not understand why May is not coming back to see me.

Yesterday for a wonder the light kept in and I lay in bed reading until 3.00am. Have also been with Nina Michaelovna to see my old friend, the dancing teacher and it brought back so many memories. Remember the past and sigh for the future they say – I suppose it is true.

9TH NOVEMBER 1917 – THURSDAY

Went out for a few minutes. It is bitingly cold and quite into winter now. There is going to be an election but there are seventeen contesting parties in all, each of them enemies. How will it end? It is 9.00am and no one is up yet. May is coming perhaps tomorrow and so will tell her what I have decided.

10TH NOVEMBER 1917 - FRIDAY

May has not arrived. I have done nothing further yet about my passport. Not been out at all today and feel very much out of humour. Now tea is ready. Mr and Mrs Kartzev have gone to bed and Toulia and I are going to preside at table by ourselves. We spend such a lot of time peeping out from the windows onto the street below these days.

11TH NOVEMBER 1917 - SATURDAY

No signs of May turning up, no phone calls, no letters. Whatever is the matter with her? I suppose nothing is very urgent out there on the Podmener Estate. Mrs Sartisson will no doubt keep her very busy, not to mention Vava.

Went to the Forrests in the evening. They say that May should return to England with me as no one knows what is going to happen here, but what she decides to do is another matter.

12TH NOVEMBER 1917 - SUNDAY

Baked bread and made some biscuits for a Sister of Mercy at the church. She has invited me to see her on Tuesday.

A most monotonous day as there has been a family quarrel. I don't know what is going to happen now, whether they are going away or not. Everything is so unsettled. I wish May would come back. No news from anyone. No one is speaking as Mrs Kartzev is too upset by argument with Mr K and the atmosphere is very tense to say the least. I think Grandfather Grigorovitch does not want them to go away to Finland again.

I decided to make some cakes for the Sister of Mercy and spent the evening with her and an officer who spoke English very well. He also sang beautifully, in a very clear tenor voice – so very sad.

I am reading *The Last Days of Pompeii* and sewing another set of serviettes for Mrs Forrest. I am going to mend my galoshes with India rubber soles and heels. Suppose I will have to ring up the Sartissons to find out why May has not arrived.

15TH NOVEMBER 1917 – WEDNESDAY

The election is going on. I expect the Bolsheviks will get in. One of Ida's admirers rang up today and says he will take me to the cinema in a few days time. He wants to know about Ida.

I have been reading to the children who are both feeling off colour and remembered a rather funny story from my childhood to tell them. Our father would take the eldest of us for a troika ride every winter. It was an exciting event as some of father's friends and their children came too. On this particular occasion we had been waiting for what seemed to me to be a very long time before the sledge and three horses set off. In those days the drivers used to shout, 'Hey! We are being robbed!' in Russian, to set the horses off at a gallop. I was so impatient and tired of waiting that I stood up and shouted this phrase in a loud voice. The horses immediately set off at a gallop. Of course, everyone was jolted forward and father's friend, a most sedate-looking man, turned suddenly and his false teeth flew out of his mouth and landed somewhere in the snow. Father was very angry with me. The driver had great difficulty in stopping the horses and we had to wait while father's friend went back to search in the snow for his false teeth. Toulia and Andrei thought this was so funny. They begged me to tell it over again. I suppose I'll have to repeat it. I think the children are going to be ill again.

16TH NOVEMBER 1917 – THURSDAY

Both children are unwell so we have been sitting indoors. Just at dinner-time this evening May rang up. We went out to the cinema and have more or less decided to go to England but May is going back to Finland on Saturday for another week.

17TH NOVEMBER 1917 – FRIDAY

I feel very excited at the thought of going back to England. I still cannot believe it is really possible if the British Consul will pay half or some of our fare.

Went to the Forrests. May was there and we had a laugh together for the first time in ages.

The Bolsheviks are now in power and no one knows what is going to happen.

18TH NOVEMBER 1917 – SATURDAY

Saw May off at the station back to Finland.

I got such a fright this afternoon as Mrs Forrest called at our house to tell me that we may become prisoners of war soon, especially if the Bolsheviks make peace with Germany. I am just waiting to hear what the Consul will say.

19TH NOVEMBER 1917 – SUNDAY

Went to see Nina Michaelovna who is going away on the 25th of this month. I will be sorry to say goodbye to them. She is still begging me to go with them. We talked about the summer we spent in Kuokkola. Sometimes I think Adia will just turn up suddenly, out of the blue, like he used to do and stop me from going away. She has not seen the Porowshin family for a long time and knows nothing about them. Piotr Petrovitch says we will all be starving to death if we stay here. Food prices are rising nearly every day now and it is quite a common sight to see carts piled with baskets and bundles heading out of the city.

20TH NOVEMBER 1917 – MONDAY

Went to the Consul and to the Moika where my papers will be ready for me in two days time. I am absolutely determined to go now.

21ST NOVEMBER 1917 – TUESDAY

I was very surprised at 7.00am to hear May on the phone asking me to meet her at the Forrests' house. She is going to prepare her papers and the Consul will pay most of our fares. It is decided that I shall take little Shura, the Forrests' son, back to England with me and deliver him to his grandmother in London. Mrs Forrest says it is for the best but she can hardly bear to part with him.

It is very frosty. I am going to start to pack all my things so that there will be no rush. I have to get all my photographs together and take them to be censored at the Finnish Station.

23RD NOVEMBER 1917 – THURSDAY

No news from anyone. Went to see the Forrests again this evening. Toulia cried so much when she knew that I was going. I went out with the children and the sledge. Wrote a letter to Natasha and Petya. Mr Grigorovitch gave me a present of some exquisite nightdresses and said how grateful he was to me for having stayed with the children. They had belonged to his wife and are far too glamorous for me.

26TH NOVEMBER 1917 – SUNDAY

It is afternoon. May has arrived back. We have been to church this morning to pray for our safe journey. Called at Mrs Forrest's this afternoon and I am going to stay at home this evening. Mrs Forrest says we must go before Christmas. We have to go to the Smolny to get permission to leave the country; it is now the Headquarters of the Bolsheviks. It seems very odd to think this place was once an elite school for daughters of the aristocracy – and where our great aunt Adelaide was educated – now occupied by the Bolsheviks intent on killing them all off.

28TH NOVEMBER 1917 – TUESDAY

Last night a very curious thing happened and we were up all night without any sleep at all. At 12.45am as I was reading in bed, heard a noise of moving furniture downstairs and many voices right under my window. I got up and peeped out, where I saw a whole crowd of Red Guards. Just then the house alarm went off and we had to dress in great haste. Got the children dressed and made them lie down then Mrs Kartzev and I began to peep out onto the street. For more than an hour we could see nothing except more Red Guards arriving and keeping guard just below my window. We live on the first floor and below there are shops, one of which used to sell bread. The shop under my room has been locked up since the war started and no one knew there was a store of wine in there.

Well, it seems that some of the soldiers got in and then more and more arrived. Some of them got in through the window. The next thing we saw was a lot of baskets of wine being brought out and put into a car. Then the Guards all stood and debated or argued I suppose about what they were going to do with it. The next minute we saw all the bottles start flying out into the street and within about five minutes well over a thousand bottles had been smashed. The snow all around turned red. Our porter says that the first lot of Red Guards stole a great many bottles and ran off with them. We were afraid they would get drunk and start to fire their guns at the houses.

Towards 5.00am they gradually drifted away and things went quiet. Next day the smell of wine permeated the house and all the snow around was red. People kept stopping to gaze at the huge expanse of saturated snow and the smashed bottles everywhere. It is truly amazing how much wine some people have in their cellars. You would never dream that just one family could store thousands of bottles of wine for years collected almost like jewellery, as in the Princess Paley household at Tsarskoe Selo where Ida said 10,000 bottles were stored. Perhaps they have smashed all those as well. Unbelievable wealth – Grand Duke Paul employed over 100 servants there. There must be a great number of drunken guards wandering about the streets and plundering the houses. No one can feel safe these days.

29TH NOVEMBER 1917 – WEDNESDAY

I went with May to the Smolny and from there to the Ministry of Foreign Affairs who then sent us to the British Consul to sign another paper. We had to wait for hours in each place but of course nothing came of it and we have to wait like prisoners, freezing cold and so tired. Hard to believe the Smolny was once a school for ladies of the aristocracy and that our own aunt Adelaide once tripped along those corridors. It is in a terrible state since the Bolsheviks took it over as their headquarters.

Spent the evening at the Forrests' house talking about what we had been through all day. It was Trotsky who came to interview us and asked the same old questions again.

'Why do you want to go?'

May was very calm and replied in her best governess manner, 'There will not be any call for governesses in the future.'

I was terribly nervous having had no sleep the night before and waiting for so long to face this ordeal.

Trotsky, who really is a forbidding looking man said, 'The British are holding two of our men. When they are released and repatriated, you may then be able to leave.'

With that, we came home very depressed and shivering. Mrs Forrest keeps giving me instructions about Shura. He is such a dear little boy; I don't know how she can bear to part with him. Now it all depends on the release of two Russians.

30TH NOVEMBER 1917 – THURSDAY

Today was Andrei's Names Day. We were out all the morning and went to church in the afternoon. After tea, Mrs Forrest rang up in a terrible state saying we must get out of the country somehow or other. She says the Bolsheviks will certainly make peace with Germany but how we are to do that if we cannot get permission I do not know. Anyway I am packing things come what may. I feel more unsettled than ever now.

1ST DECEMBER 1917 – FRIDAY

We have been to the British Consulate again but they sent us back to the Office of Foreign Affairs where we left our passports. They say they will let us know something next week. There is a great deal more trouble to be got through somehow before we are finally allowed to go. This evening we spent at the Forrest's. May is going back to Finland tomorrow morning to pack her things. The Forrests have decided that they are going to the south. I wish they were coming to England with us. No letters from anyone.

2ND DECEMBER 1917 – SATURDAY

This morning Mrs Kartzev and I went to the Jews' market to sell two coats. Wine fumes are everywhere in the town and all the cellars are being robbed. It is a very funny sight to see wine being pumped out into the streets and the snow turning red. A lot of the Red Guards are staggering about and no one knows whether they will shoot. If anyone tries to stop them they are shot on the spot and no one takes any notice.

Yesterday, on my way to meet May, I witnessed a shooting on our street and never thought anything about it. People did not run. No one took any notice. The Red Guards make bonfires at their numerous sentry posts where they sit around with their guns at the ready.

I am staying at home tonight but tomorrow will go to the Forrests and she will introduce me to an officer who is going to England.

3RD DECEMBER 1917 – SUNDAY

People say that there is going to be a big fight in Petrograd. I hope I am not here to see it. Today, I bumped into our old friend, poor, old Miss Elizabeth Waters who lives on the outskirts of town. She is also trying to get away to England. She has been a governess all her life. Her employer is going to India and wants her to accompany him. He has been in love with her for a long time but she says she is going to Manchester, to find her sister and niece. She has the deeds or what pass for deeds to her house and is trying to sell it, without much success. I don't think anyone will want to buy houses here in future.

She was one of a large family living in Manchester and was adopted by some people who were coming to live in Russia when she was only four years old. Her English speech is very broken and jumbled.

In the evening I went to the Forrests. There were two officers there and we talked about England. The lovely musical evenings which Mrs Forrest used to hold are a thing of the past now. Everyone talks about going away.

4TH DECEMBER 1917 – MONDAY

As we were walking today we heard shooting somewhere very near. A few people started to run but we continued walking. I think we must get used to the sound of shooting and try to continue with our own lives. May is coming back on Wednesday and will stay with the Forrests. The Bolsheviks have taken all the motorcars and so Mr Forrest no longer has a job.

The Montashov brothers have gone back to their oil wells in Armenia as far as I know and the Morskaya houses look deserted. I did not see Adia's mother after all, but asked Nina Michaelovna what she knew about him. All she could say was that he is still alive. Who knows what happened or why he stopped writing to me. I don't know. People are just disappearing from the town every day.

Went to have our photograph albums checked and stamped; trembling in case they found the ones of Rasputin and the Tsarina. There was a long queue of very nervous people and it did not seem possible that they would go through every photograph. Some of the pages were stuck together purposely; they flicked through the lot very quickly and I was back out on the street breathing a sigh of relief before I knew it, thank God.

5TH DECEMBER 1917 – TUESDAY

I am so upset about everything that I can hardly write. Mrs Forrest and I went to sell some things, wandered about – queues everywhere. Some of the shops have a secret password before you can even enter. I have spent the whole evening at home thinking and wondering about whether we will get our passports.

6TH DECEMBER 1917 – WEDNESDAY

Went to sell some more things. People are selling clothes because they fetch such good prices and even old, patched underclothes are snatched up quickly. May arrived back in town and we went to the Office of Foreign Affairs and got permission to go at last but tomorrow we have to go to the Consulate again.

7TH DECEMBER 1917 – THURSDAY

We had such an awful day. We stood in the Consulate for 3 hours. We can now go any time after next Monday. I am taking Shura back with me to England. They say it is a terrible boat journey over to Sweden. May is staying at the Forrest's but I have come home to pack. I came back before 9.00pm but have done nothing yet. We were under fire all day and it makes one feel very nervous. I still cannot believe that we are going – actually going – to England and will see mother again after seven long years have passed away. I have three suitcases and one rather large hatbox. I am packing my Russian costume and will do the Russian dance for mother when I get home.

1918

After being at home for over three weeks, I can start to write my diary once again although cannot write down all that has happened. We had an awful, long journey of 18 days. Some of the passengers on the boat had bloated stomachs due to starvation and they were very ill. Miss Waters, our friend, was also travelling with us. She was wearing a wadded coat – the wadding packed with rouble notes. She thinks she will be able to change them in England. Everyone looked yellow because their diets have been comprised mainly of cabbage and were wearing what can only be described as rags. We landed in Scotland where even those Russians who could speak English could not understand a word of what the Scottish porters and people were saying to them. May had to do some translating a few times for various groups of bemused people, who just stood there wondering what language they were speaking.

Miss Waters was going to Manchester to find her sister whom she had not seen since she was four years old. I had a rest at home for a week before I took little Shura Forrest down to London to stay with his grandmother. The poor little boy looked bewildered when I left him there as he does not speak or understand much English. It was very nice to see some of the sights of London but the weather was bad and I was glad to get back home.

Mother looks much older of course but I was hugged to death by everyone. Ella, Ida and Vara came from Lancaster, where they have been working in a munitions factory and we spent a very jolly time. Now, I have only to see my brother Leslie but I shall have to wait until Easter for that. Father is greatly changed – not quite as talkative as he was but seems very pleased and glad to see us all together once more and happy to be able to converse with us in Russian again. There were too many questions to answer at first and it was so exciting.

May and I have started to practise shorthand as we both intend to get jobs in offices of some kind. Up to the present, we have not heard of anything – we just hope to do so soon.

I have not had any news at all from Russia and don't suppose I shall as the state of affairs there is dreadful.

5TH FEBRUARY 1918 – TUESDAY

It feels very strange to be writing in my diary again – in fact everything is a bit strange now though I expect I shall get used to it. The day passed very slowly. I had a letter from Mrs Blount, Shura's grandmother, to say that he is quite well. I am again getting used to the old routine at home – Friday is cleaning day, Saturday is baking day. It is very gloomy and pours with rain. We practise our shorthand and have borrowed a typewriter to practise typing on.

Ida is really quiet when she is here but we had a lot to talk about between ourselves. Father has told us not to mention Rasputin to anyone, nor to talk about Aunt Verubova. Before the end of 1917 Ida received a telegram from Alexander Pistolkors asking her to meet him at a London hotel. It was worded in such an urgent way she decided to go and ask for any news of May and myself. Pistolkors turned up in his British officers uniform immaculate to the last detail. He described how his three little daughters, Sandra, Olga and Tatiana, were heartbroken without her and cried constantly for her return. Aylia, who had been used to two nursemaids as well as a governess, could not pacify them and was completely unable to cope with three small children. He offered to provide whatever she wanted if only she would consider returning to Copenhagen with him.

Hunted by the Bolsheviks, Pistolkors was by this time a very desperate man. Although quite safe in his British officer's uniform, here was a man who had already faced a Red Army firing squad and more recently been involved in plots to rescue the Tsar, also his stepfather Grand Duke Paul and mother, Princess Paley. With his commanding officer, Colonel Locker Lampson, he had planned to smuggle a British army uniform into Tsarskoe Selo, in which the Tsar would be disguised, taken to a waiting ambulance and onto a train going north to Archangel. A similar plan was devised for his stepfather but both refused to take part in it since neither wished to leave their families in the hands of the Bolsheviks. When the plan was discovered, Pistolkors made his escape to Stockholm.

6TH FEBRUARY 1918 – WEDNESDAY

We are going to the Labour Exchange. No sign of any work as yet. We went to see one of our aunts, then to the cinema.

8TH FEBRUARY 1918 – FRIDAY

Cleaning day. We cleaned the house until late in the afternoon. It was raining cats and dogs. This evening we have been to the cinema again. I am writing a letter to Nina Michaelovna but wonder whether she will ever receive it.

Baking day, made bread and pies. It's raining as usual. May and I fall into the routine of weekly household tasks with each day dedicated to some kind of cleaning, washing, cooking or polishing – I will have to get used to it. Ida came home late tonight; she is the most maternal of all of us and is still very upset about leaving the family in Copenhagen. A letter from Ida's friend Count Komorovsky arrived today with news of Anna Verubova who had spent three months in the notorious prison Peter and Paul Fortress. Whilst in the prison she was examined by doctors who pronounced that she was still a virgin. This came as a great surprise to many people who believed she was more than a close friend of Rasputin. On her release she had gone to her sister's ransacked apartment on Morskaya street only to be turned away by Alexander Pistolkors and his sister Marianne. No one is willing to take her in fear that the Red Guards may come to arrest her – which they did – and charged her with being a 'counter revolutionary'. She was sent to the naval station prison on the island of Sveborg in the Bay of Helsinfors, where she remained for another 4 months before being released. Forced into hiding, she resumed her maiden name of Taneyeva. This news was quite shocking for Ida, who had spent so many hours with Anna and the children and knew how childish and naïve she was with an absolute unshakeable belief in Rasputin's power to heal. Treated like another daughter by the Tsarina, she had spent most of her life surrounded by exotic flowers, children and servants. To think of her now hobbling about the streets of Petrograd on a crutch, dressed in rags, begging for food and a floor to sleep on seemed beyond belief. The letter from Komorovski brought back such memories I am going to start writing my diary in Russian. I feel more Russian than English now I am here; small wonder that Ida is reluctant to talk about her life in Petrograd or write any letters, so I forgive her for not writing to me when she arrived home last year.

11TH FEBRUARY 1918 – MONDAY

Washing day – did our shorthand practice, then we went for a walk. In the evening we went to the cinema with mother and aunt. It is boring but there is nothing I can do about it. A letter from Leslie came to say he is well – thank God.

Not such good news about father. He came home today very sad because they told him at work that he was no longer needed. He has been working as a lift-man at the big engineering works, Platts, but he will no doubt find something else to do.

Tomorrow we have to be up early as we have to do more washing. Mother has bronchitis.

12TH–20TH FEBRUARY 1918

Cannot write very much. Nothing is new. Father is still at home, as are May and I. There are no letters from Russia for me and that is not surprising as the Russians are going to make peace with the Germans. We can hardly believe it. I would like to know what happened to the English people who stayed in Russia and what would Piotr Petrovitch say about it?

Mother is quite ill and coughing badly. Father goes out into the street to smoke his pipe. I am in such low spirits. We hear nothing about finding a job and want so much to start working. I wonder when the war will end. There is no good news.

21ST FEBRUARY 1918 – THURSDAY

It is quite difficult to get provisions now and sometimes there are queues but not like in Russia for butter, meat and bread. So far it is not too bad, but who knows when the war will come to an end? I am afraid to think about it. Will it ever end? Yesterday,

I almost went to sign on for a women's regiment in the army but they wanted a good typist and am not yet very quick at it, otherwise I would sign up immediately and go to France. So now have to wait until I can do the shorthand and typing much more quickly. Our cousin promised to ask someone she knows who needs a stenographer – this is the word she uses – and will let me know.

22ND FEBRUARY 1918 – FRIDAY

Cleaning day. Today we cleaned all the rooms. After dinner I wrote six letters and now it is 10.00pm. I will get so fat through sitting too much. We still have no young friends and therefore it is very boring. Adia, poor boy! I left him to his fate and will probably never see him again. Life is so strange. One meets people and then parts with them forever. Today I am in such low spirits again thinking of the past. Something always seems to be wrong with me. Tomorrow is the same monotonous programme. Baking day. I will be busy and in this way the time will pass more quickly. Well, it is better than to sit and think.

23RD FEBRUARY 1918 – SATURDAY

It was the normal boring day I'm sorry to say. In the evening we went to dinner at our cousin's. May and I might possibly go to a dance where there will be many soldiers from the hospital.

1ST MARCH 1918 – FRIDAY

I skipped five days as there was nothing much to write about. We have been busy on the typewriter – a lot of practice at typing letters of the 'Dear Sir' variety. Yesterday we went to a dance. It was not very interesting because it took so long to get there. We were late arriving and all the girls had their dance cards full.

On Tuesday Ella came to visit. She says it is good in Lancaster and she likes it very much. She has a lot of friends there. She went back yesterday after dinner.

May received a letter today to say that she is hired for a job and will earn 30 shillings a week at first which will increase later on. It is a good beginning. Father also went to apply for another job. I hope he will be lucky. Now I am the only one left at home.

2ND MARCH 1918 – SATURDAY

This morning, would you believe, I got a letter about a place where I went for an interview. They asked me to write a letter which I have done but still do not know whether I will get the job.

Father got a job yesterday but it is too far away and we don't know how he will manage to travel. We are going to a cinema tonight as usual.

3RD MARCH 1918 – SUNDAY

We were at home all day long. I have received a letter about a job at last and start to work for an accountant next Wednesday so am furiously practising my shorthand and typing.

6TH MARCH 1918 – WEDNESDAY

I am so terribly tired tonight. I started work in an office. There is another girl there who seems friendly. So far it is alright but it's too soon to make judgements and am hurrying this because I have to bang on the typewriter now.

8TH MARCH 1918 – FRIDAY

They send us out from the office to the mills to check their accounts. It is a most boring job. I am very tired.

9TH MARCH 1918 – SATURDAY

Today I was sent to collect rents together with another girl immediately after I arrived at the office and will have to do this every Friday and Saturday. I am working all the days now except Sunday and every day is much the same.

Father is also working very late. He only gets home at about 10.00pm and is very tired. I think he will find something closer to home or try to.

11TH MARCH 1918 – MONDAY

I have worked all day and am terribly tired. Our boss is such an autocratic, pompous man. He is so irritable, has no patience and snaps out orders all the time. Today had to type out 10 letters making two copies of each one, leaving space for his signature at the bottom. At least, that is what I though he said. I finished this job and put the letters in very neat piles without a single mistake. When he came marching in, he took one look at them, then in an awful rage threw the whole lot up into the air. As they came floating down over my head, he shouted, 'You haven't the brains of a flea.' No one, not even father, has ever spoken to me like this before and I had worked so hard to get them done quickly. I stifled my tears.

'How can I have any brains, Mr B, when you have them all?' I asked and started to pick up the sheets of paper from the floor. It turned out that I had not left enough room for four signatures at the bottom of the letters. Any more cheeky answers from me and I will have the sack. I had to do the lot again and it was well after closing time when I finished. There are two girls in the office, who look like frightened little mice. I don't think anyone has ever answered him back before. I will most probably have to leave at the end of the week.

12TH MARCH 1918 – TUESDAY

A letter came from little Shura's grandmother who says that he is not well and is missing his mother. He speaks Russian all the time and she doesn't understand. What am I to do? I cannot take time off to go to London again, though I would like to. Another terrible day at the office.

'Do you know the meaning of the word alacrity?' he asked me before I was hardly in my seat at the desk. Although my English is not perfect and sometimes I mix up certain words with Russian, I do have quite a good vocabulary and I told him that of course I knew it.

'Well why don't you practise it?' he snapped. Such a pompous little man with a thin face and beady eyes darting everywhere. I did not reply.

13TH MARCH 1918 – WEDNESDAY

Father is absolutely determined that neither he nor any of us will work in the cotton mills. I don't know why he is so determined not to. He prefers to do odd jobs like working in a warehouse but he can't find anything nearer home just now. The doctor says mother has chronic bronchitis. It seems she has it every winter.

Our house is in the centre of town. On the opposite corner lower down the street is the Star Inn, a very busy public house. Father goes and stands outside there sometimes to smoke his pipe. He doesn't go in, just stands outside and talks to some of the people he knows. On the other side is the Grand Theatre where a lot of music hall stars have appeared. Mother and her two sisters go there every Friday or Saturday night. Father calls them the Three Graces, after a very popular statue by a sculptor called Canova. He can still smile at them as they go out chattering and talking. You cannot help but feel sorry for him. All his family went to Chile from Russia in about 1898; his mother and father died out there. He had at least five brothers and two sisters; one, Uncle Edward, writes to him occasionally from a place called 'Lautaro'. where he and his wife, a Chilean woman called Elvira, own a general store. Father always dreamed of going there to join his family.

14TH MARCH 1918 – THURSDAY

There are no letters from Russia and no news. They say that there is a Counter-Revolution there now.

I have been to the dentist and will have to go a few more times. My teeth ache so much.

16TH MARCH 1918 – SATURDAY

We went for a walk this evening and then to the cinema. I am longing to know what is happening in Petrograd and how everyone is going on but no one is writing to me.

This morning we were sent out to collect rents in long streets of little houses with only two windows and a door opening onto the pavement. A very strange thing happened as we entered one of these houses. There was a big photograph on the wall of a sailor in uniform and hanging from the frame was a tobacco pouch. It was one of the leather ones I made and sent to the sailors. I recognised it at once and asked the woman about it. Her son had died in the war not many months previously, so she spoke of him with tears pouring down her cheeks but she said the tobacco pouch was one of the nicest things he had received and that because he liked it so much she had hung it onto the picture frame. 'It was from a lady in Russia,' she said.

This incident I could not forget. All day I was thinking how strange it was that I should visit the house where he had lived. I stood gazing at the portrait of the smiling young sailor and was immediately taken back to Christmas 1916. How many of those leather pouches did I make? Adia's smiling face came back to me. Was it Arcardi Dmitrich smiling out at me through the portrait? What seemed like a long silence followed then I said how sorry I was and stepped out into the cold, empty street, hardly aware of anything but the sailor's smiling face.

'Mr Boss', as I call him, was in his usual bad temper when I got back and informed me that we had been out of the office wandering around the town far too long and would have to make up the time.

18TH MARCH 1918 – MONDAY

Went to work and am gradually getting more used to it but do not like it very much and I am very tired in the evening. No news from Russia – they have all forgotten me. I wish I knew what happened to Arcardi Dmitrich.

19TH MARCH 1918 – TUESDAY

Such a boring day. Went to the dentist again. No news from Russia. They have all forgotten me.

20TH MARCH 1918 – WEDNESDAY

Another monotonous day at the office. There is very bad news from the war as the Germans are on the offensive. I am so tired that I cannot write any more.

23RD MARCH 1918 – SATURDAY

We went for a long walk about ten miles and came home very tired. It is going to be a sad Easter I think. Mother is recovering very slowly but cannot do very much. I get used to my work little by little and am now much quicker at shorthand.

24TH MARCH 1918 – SUNDAY

A very boring day spent at home and have no news from anyone. It is raining cats and dogs. Easter here is quite boring, not like the happy times we used to have in Russia so I am not looking forward to it. My work continues but cannot say I like it. After a little while I can perhaps find a better place where they will pay higher wages. I wish I knew what happened to Arcardi Dmitritch, and where they all went to and what has happened to them. Next weekend will be Easter Sunday. Ida, Vara and Ella are coming home. The only one missing will be Leslie who cannot get any leave. We will no doubt say *Kristos Voskres* amongst ourselves and I might even bake an Easter cake. At least we will all be together again. The Bolsheviks have signed a treaty with the Germans, the 'Brest-Litovsk Treaty', and are no longer at war with Germany. I am sure that Piotr Petrovitch with his long family tradition of army life must be devastated. The Germans will keep the territories they have already occupied, in Poland, the Baltic and regions around the Caucuses and Byelorussia. I wonder where Arcardi Dmitritch is? Nina Michaelovna Loukina must be in Tiflis and knows nothing about him otherwise I think she would have written to me.

Am I turning into another Munya Golovina, mourning the death of a lover for the rest of my life? Ida and I used to think she was very silly but how I long to have letters and news from Adia like I used to. I still have his Russian christening cross. I don't wear it because it reminds me so much of the past. Now I have to think of the future somehow, and try to forget the past.

25TH MARCH 1918 – MONDAY

My work continues but cannot say I like it very much. Perhaps after a little while I might be able to find another place. There are a lot of 'social evenings' advertised in the local newspaper asking for people to entertain – singing, dancing or reciting monologues – to raise money for the war effort. Maybe I'll go and do my Russian dance. I unpacked my Russian dance costume tonight and pressed it. When mother is better I will dance for her.

26TH MARCH 1918 – TUESDAY

Another long day at the office. 'Mr Boss' is at my elbow, looking at his watch, telling me I am too slow. In the evening I put on the Russian dance costume intending to practice a few steps but there is very little room in this small bedroom I share with Ida and May. After a few minutes father was shouting from downstairs that he thought the ceiling was coming down. I think my dancing days are over.

27TH MARCH 1918 – WEDNESDAY

There is no one among our English acquaintances who knows very much about Russia or can understand how closely we were involved with the families we worked for. Questions about the Bolsheviks and Rasputin we are not able to discuss as father says it is not 'suitable conversation for three young girls in mixed company'. Whatever we say seems to be a real conversation stopper and I'm sure nobody believes us anyway. Ida was talking about the Grand Duchess Maria when we visited our cousins the other day. Complete silence descended – I suppose we will have to get used to it.

28TH MARCH 1918 – THURSDAY

At last a letter arrived for May from Vava and Mrs Sartisson which was passed around between us and I'm copying it into my diary so that I will never forget what happened to them.

Dearest Deakie

How I miss you. How could you leave me? I hope you have a lot to eat. We are nearly starving here. I wish I was with you in England. I have not received one single letter from you. We are now staying at Uncle Fedia's lodging in Petrograd because ours is too expensive for us. The Red Guards came to our house in

Terijoki nearly every day and took things away. Please write a letter to the little girl you left behind. Do not forget me. I have not forgotten you. Mother is writing also.

Best love and kisses from Vava

My dear Deakie

You cannot imagine what we had to go through here. My husband is still trying to find work and hopes to succeed in a little business. My nerves have become quite senseless. The Red Guards plundered everything in Terijoki – even 'Palmira' Vava's pony. In Petrograd life was so expensive and not to be hungry we had to spend at least 100 roubles a day. Our apartment in Petrograd is now a hospital; we had to sell everything and we 'ate' all the money from the sale – yes we ate all of it. We have moved to Uncle Fedia's (my husband's brother). We tried to escape to Riga taking only what we could carry; we travelled in a cart with 15 other people and slept in one small room. I did not undress for 13 days. But we had only enough money for one month so had to return from Riga, once again a terrible journey. I was so seasick and ill. How glad I was to see the lights of Helsingfors. We are now staying in Vammelsum; I had to leave my precious photo albums and I don't expect to see the few things we left with friends, or all my jewellery left with our estate manager. It is a great question if it still exists. Some people have made the very dangerous and perilous journey to Germany which cost them as much as 3 million roubles. Very lucky they had it. My husband is doing his best to find work. Please tell me how you and your sisters are getting on and give them our regards. We anxiously await your letters.

Best love, Ludmilla Sartisson

We discussed this letter sitting up very late until after midnight and realise how lucky we were to have escaped from Petrograd.

2ND APRIL 1918 – TUESDAY

The Easter weekend passed quietly; mother is still recovering from bronchitis and only gets up in the afternoon – but we were together – something I had dreamed of for so long. We had an Easter cake and it was so strange when we all sat down together, even father remarked on the fact that we five girls are now quite 'grown up'. Although the war is still on things are not as we remembered. Most of the young men are away at the war including our brother Leslie; we must be thankful for small mercies. We moved the table in the front room and I did the Russian dance for mother. We have a gramophone and May has managed to get some records of Chaliapin singing (in Russian) 'The Volga Boatmen' and 'The Flea' which our father likes, also music for the dance – she went shopping to Manchester for these. Father knows both these songs and can give quite a good rendition of 'The Flea' and of course loves Chaliapin the great Russian baritone. We have quite a collection of his Russian books here as well as Chekov and Dostoevski which were brought back from Petersburg in 1905. He doesn't forget the Russian language at all since he was brought up with it like we were.

6TH APRIL 1918 – SATURDAY

Today I received a postcard from Natasha written in English; just three short sentences.

Dear Miss Daisy

How bad you are to go away from us. Mama cries well. And so do I. And so does Petya. Goodbye.

From your Natasha

At least there is an address on it – so I can reply to Tiflis. Nina Michaelovna refused to speak any English whilst I was there so I expect she also refused to write any. It's very brave for little Natasha, who is only 8 years old to write in English.

7TH APRIL 1918 – SUNDAY

True to old habits I sit up late at night writing letters and filling in my diary. Last night I wrote to Natasha and Nina Michaelovna. Today's newspapers were full of the news that the Bolsheviks have signed a peace treaty with Germany, the 'Brest-Litovsk armistice'. How much I long to have letters and news from Adia like I used to. I still have his Russian christening cross with the words 'Save and Guard'. I don't wear it because it reminds so much of the past. I left without goodbyes to him.

This weekend we saw an advert in one of the newspapers for girls who can sing and dance. Auditions are to be held at a theatre in Manchester. I might possibly go there and see if anything comes of it. Ida said she would come with me. We would have to make some excuse to father. He has got a job in a warehouse but it is so far away he does not get home until 10.00pm and he is very tired by this time. He is so old fashioned, 'No daughter of mine is going on the stage,' he said. He is quite adamant once he has given an order and expects us to follow it without question.

8TH APRIL 1918 – MONDAY

A hard day at work though I am much quicker at shorthand than I was at first. The audition is next Saturday so I am practising my dance at night. Ida will come home Friday night, so can think of nothing else at the moment.

13TH APRIL 1918 – SATURDAY

Father was working today so we had no trouble in setting off to Manchester with my costume in a bag. The audition was at 11.00am – but had to wait an hour for my turn to go on. I got a lot of applause from the group who were watching and was told later on that I had actually got a job in the chorus of some musical show they were putting on and will have to present myself in a month's time. Ida asked how was I going to tell father. I will try to tell him when he is in a good mood as soon as possible.

14TH APRIL 1918 – SUNDAY

Two of mother's sisters and their husbands came to visit this afternoon, so we were very busy preparing food. Father warned us not to mention anything about Rasputin – and that we must not talk about Russia too much. He still treats us like children. I had no opportunity to tell him about the audition. We do not go to church very often here; father is very much against any religious beliefs now as are many people who have lost sons in the war. Mother has 4 sisters living close by who visit us quite often and she likes to go out with them to the theatre. The Grand Theatre is only a few minutes away from where we live and when she is well enough they often go there on Friday or Saturday night. Sometimes I go with them and am at the moment learning to do an imitation of Vesta Tilley – who is very well known here – in fact I can do imitations of all the music hall stars once I have learnt the songs – I will have to tell father tomorrow about the audition.

16TH APRIL 1918 – WEDNESDAY

A postcard came from Elizabeth Waters asking me to call and see her. She is living in a house somewhere behind Picadilly station in Manchester – I will probably go on Saturday afternoon. I intend to tell father about the audition on Sunday when he is rested and in a peaceful mood. Went to see poor old Miss Waters living in a very dilapidated house in the back streets behind the station. Found it eventually at the end of a long row of 'two-up two-down' houses with doors opening onto the street; it had once been a corner shop. She was renting a room from a man whose wife was an invalid, completely crippled with arthritis.

As Miss Waters opened the door a very loud noise of rattling tin-cans began. The empty cans, labels removed, hung shining and silvery from a string attached to the front door and looped around the room on nails in the wall. The room was quite empty with bare floorboards. 'A very good burglar alarm', she explained in Russian. She speaks such broken English no one can understand her.

In the next room an old woman lay on a bed in the corner, propped up with dirty pillows and cushions. Her hands were so deformed she looked like an old witch. She was smoking a cigarette clipped onto the end of a stick which she could barely hold, so badly crippled were her hands. After a very broken conversation in English, Miss Waters took me upstairs to her bedroom where there was just a single iron bedstead, a chest of drawers and a chair. From under the bed she pulled out a big suitcase which when opened revealed thousands of Russian rouble notes tightly packed into it which she is hoping to exchange for English money. There were 23,000 Russian roubles altogether.

She wondered if I could help her write a letter to the 'General Council for the Assistance of British Repatriated from Russia' – whose president was 'The Honourable Sir G Buchanan HCB', vice-president Lady Sydenham'. Sir George Buchanan was the British Ambassador in Petrograd and had done seven years service there. He was made an honorary citizen of Moscow in 1916 and given a priceless icon. I remembered he once dined at the Admiralty with Ivan Constantin Grigorovitch. I was taken aback by the amount of money she had managed to smuggle (all stuffed into the wadding of her coat) and now quite worthless in England. I don't think I had ever seen so much money before in my life – I suppose this was the reason for the tin-cans at the door. The value in English money would be around £12,000 – a huge amount. She was also trying to claim on a house she had bought in 1915, a few miles from Petrograd. There was no proper address for it she said. When I asked her she said, 'From Petrograd one goes by the Nicholas station to the station Popovka and it is the second road from there, house number 32, also some land, 400 sagens with well and sheds (7 English feet = 1 sagen) and it is worth about 8,000 roubles. I suppose the Red Guards have taken it by this time.'

She looked so pathetic standing there in that cold, barely furnished little bedroom; a tiny, bird-like little woman with wire spectacles and thin wispy, grey hair scraped backed into a bun, trying to earn a living somehow. True to her English governess stock-in-trade, 'never sit with idle hands', she made children's toys and patchwork blankets, working with scraps of material and wool she managed to scrounge from somewhere. When she arrived here she found her sister had died and her niece and children had emigrated to Canada. Her former employer in Petrograd had escaped to India, a very wealthy man whose wife died leaving him with three children. He had proposed marriage to her and written to her from India begging her to join him there. She refused to go, thinking she would find family of her own here in Manchester.

Sitting on her bed we composed a letter to Sir George Buchanan, will get it typed in the office and come back to see her again.

21ST APRIL 1918 – SUNDAY

We had a lot of housework to do today and I am too tired to write. Father was unapproachable as usual.

May received another letter from Vava, which we read avidly, together. No one understands how much we long to hear from the children we left behind. I am sure they do not understand and seem to think we deserted them, poor things.

Dearest Deakie

We got at last your letter. I could not help crying as everything in it reminded me of the good life we had when you were with us. You tell us to leave the country but how to do it when we have no money? My father is in Copenhagen with his brother, Uncle Fedia. We may move to Viborg as he does not want us to remain here long so near to the frontier. We have also got a permit for Switzerland but I don't think we will go there as the exchange is so bad. We can get for 600 Finnish marks only 60 Swiss francs. I am reading 'Gulliver's Travels' and like it very much. Write and tell me if you have lovers like Mr Cummings and if you are getting married. Mother has heard nothing from the people where Miss Daisy was and has no idea where they went to. Please write to me very soon. Best love and kisses.

From Vava.

It seems that Vava is growing up very quickly now May is no longer with her. What will happen to them now they have no money left I wonder?

There don't seem to be any opportunities of finding a better job here. After all Oldham is a cotton mill town and nearly every job here is connected in some way to the mills. There are hundreds of them scattered in all the surrounding towns as well. From a distance the town looks like a forest of tall mill chimneys, all belching thick clouds of smoke and nearly everyone is employed in the mills. Father flatly refused to get a job in the mill though he could very easily have done so. Since most of the able-bodied younger men are away at the war more and more women are employed. Also very young girls of no more than 12 years are taken on as they are able to crawl under the machines to clean up. They are called 'little part-timers' and do half a day at school and half a day at the mill. They all seem to wear long skirts with grey or brown shawls over their heads and shoulders and clogs which make such a loud noise when they all come out of the mills at the same time. Make sure you are never on the street walking in the opposite direction or you would just be swept away by them.

Of course mother and her sisters are quite familiar with this town as they came here as young girls from Liverpool to find work when their father died. Our father seems to be the odd one out and however little money we have prefers to find odd jobs in warehouses and such like. He is now quite recovered from being an alcoholic and never touches a drop. He could hardly afford to now. We are all very glad that he has recovered of course. Mother is totally dependant on the wages that we sisters bring in and I suppose it is quite frivolous and selfish of me to think of going off to dance in a chorus-line somewhere. I must tell father about it this week sometime.

28TH APRIL 1918 – SUNDAY

I plucked up enough courage and approached father this afternoon. I should have known better. He immediately flew into a temper and said I was not even to think of it. He thinks I will turn into a 'floosie'. 'Do you want to turn into some kind of floosie, prancing on stage every night because that is exactly what will happen to you and no daughter of mine is going to do that. You might just as well start walking the streets. Don't even think about accepting the job. Just sit down now and write a letter telling them you are not going to accept it, and that's the end of it', he said.

I could see that there was very little point in arguing with him – though I did try. In the end I just gave up. Ida and May tried to pacify things; mother hummed a little tune and tapped her fingers on the table. A black cloud descended for the rest of the day so I stayed in the bedroom out of the way for a long time wondering what to do.

29TH APRIL 1918 – MONDAY

Letters are beginning to come through but take along time to get here. Mrs Sartisson's letter to May was posted in Sweden; perhaps she sent it to her husband to post from there. I don't think they trust anyone in Petrograd now. All the officers had to strip off their epaulettes and any decorations by order of the Bolsheviks or they were torn off by the Red Guards. So I imagine this happened to Piotr Petrovitch as well – I am sure Adia would have managed to get my address somehow and written to me by this time.

Another letter arrived for May from Mrs Sartisson to say that Mr Sartisson was coming to England as he cannot find any work there in Sweden. It contained only bad news, news I did not want to hear.

Dearest Deakie

We were so happy to receive your letter. My sister Vera is in Switzerland somewhere but we don't know where. I am trying to sell part of the estate now as it is too great an expense for me, especially at present as we are already in debt. All the villas here have been robbed by the Red Guards. Alas the Podmener estate, which my father built with is own hands, is no more. With his last Danish crowns my husband left for England hoping to find his luck there. He is staying with 'Miss Deakon', my old English governess when I was a child, and of course your namesake. We now have a little hope our good English friends will help him find a job at last.

Forgive me for writing about money matters but at the present moment we have to count every penny. We have to be very economical to pay our debts. When I think of how I used to love spending money before and now I dislike it so much. If you only knew how sorry I was to part with all our furniture and the things so dear to me. But there was no other way. We had to give up our apartment in Petrograd. It is a hospital now.

I hope my husband's services will be valuable in England, but there are lots of engineers in your country also looking for work. I am not sure that I would like to live in a country where the climate is so bad and the houses so terribly inconvenient and cold. We sold everything except Vava's big cupboard in order to survive. Please tell me how your sisters are and give them our regards. We anxiously await your letters.

Best love from Ludmilla Sartisson.

PS. We have heard through an ex-officer of the Guards regiment that the person you were asking about, 'Arcardi Dmitrich Porowshin', was reported to be 'missing in action' early this year and nothing further is known of him.

EPILOGUE

Memories of my mother and her sisters remain very clear because they all lived to a great old age and were very fond of sitting round the kitchen table 'til all hours of the night reminiscing about old times.

When grandfather died (1935) May and Ida decided to move to Cleveleys and run a small boardinghouse, hoping the clear air would cure grandmother's bronchitis. Cleveleys, a short distance up the coast from Blackpool, was in those days an undeveloped little resort with sand dunes and grass on the sea front, quite unlike the popular, noisy Blackpool.

Their Russian background slowly faded into the past but every so often something would happen to jog their memories out of Lancashire back to Russia when newspaper reports about the marriage ceremony of some exiled Russian prince Ida had known were published or when odd letters began to filter through from Nina Michaelovna. But there was much to amuse them in Lancashire, such as the cotton mill manager who came back to Oldham from Petersburg with a Russian bride who spoke hardly a word of English and became 'Mrs Winterbottom'.

The boardinghouse had three storeys, overlooked the sea and was where we spent holidays. It became a meeting place for friends and family where most of the talking and gossiping went on in the kitchen.

The Second World War started soon after they moved to Cleveleys. Our visits continued intermittently by saving up petrol coupons and food rations and then quite suddenly after the war ended May received news from Vava. She was about to arrive on an Easter visit from Paris where she and her mother were living. They had spent many years of wandering in Europe – from Stockholm to Copenhagen and Berlin where her father had been desperately trying to find work. After he died they settled in Paris where Mrs Sartisson made a meagre living by giving piano lessons and, as May later found out, Vava had become an expensive escort to visiting tourists. Because of their Jewish background they had spent over a year in a German concentration camp in occupied France. Married and divorced years previously Vava was now 42 years old.

There was great excitement amongst the sisters as they gathered to witness this link with their past. After years of austerity during the war, Vava appeared like a creature from another planet with her beautiful clothes, perfect features, ash blond hair, her strange broken English and an air of fading beauty. She had not forgotten anything of her English training with May, she said:

'Just imagine Deakie, most of my friends don't even know how many days in the month there are! Yet I remember us sitting in the nursery reciting, '30 days has September, April, June and November, – and do you remember Deakie, how I used to throw my hair brushes at you!'

Ida was always anxious to hear any small piece of news about the Pistolkors family and their relations in spite of the fact that it sent cold shivers down her spine. Vava told them how she had seen both Dmitri Pavlovitch and Aylia when she was living in Copenhagen. 'It must have been in 1920 when I saw Dmitri Pavlovitch in a restaurant having dinner with the wife of the British ambassador, Sir Charles Manning. Dmitri was still in mourning for his father Grand duke Paul and his stepbrother

Vladimir.' From various news reports Ida already knew the fate of these two men whom she and Daisy had seen many times at the numerous names day and Christmas parties held for the children in Tsarskoe Selo and at the Pistolkors apartments.

Grand duke Paul was shot at the Fortress of Peter and Paul where he had been imprisoned; Vladimir (who was just 21 years old) and the Tsarina's sister Ella were taken to Alapaevsk, a short distance from Ekaterinburg in Siberia, to a place where there were some deserted coal mines. They were thrown into one of the pits followed by stones and logs and a great number of grenades and dynamite. It was said the guards could still hear hymn singing long afterwards from the depths of the pit. 'Later on', Vava continued, 'I saw Aylia. She was dining at the same restaurant with the British ambassador and seemed to be very enamoured by him.'

Vava was now working for a wealthy businessman, aptly named Monsieur Riches. Following in May's footsteps she had taken a course in typing and said that the long hours spent working in his offices were compensated by holidays in Monte Carlo and Biarritz which he insisted were essential for her health.

It was hard not to notice how she treated the boardinghouse like some kind of spa hotel, so many baths – hot and cold – were taken, followed by olive oil massages, exercises and a brief walk along the seafront. Wrapped in an extravagant silk kimono, all her clothes were meticulously pressed every day and carried back and forth on hangers. The ironing board took up quite a lot of space in the busy kitchen and May's frustration became even more apparent when she discovered the two inches of cream at the top of the milk bottles had disappeared when she came downstairs. 'Why had they never thought of coming to England?' May asked her. 'The houses here are so inconvenient with their tiny fireplaces and endless shovels of coal, mother would never have considered it' she said.

The idyllic life on the Terijoki estate was recalled in vivid detail by all the sisters and the beautiful little child May had known and loved so many years ago was forgiven. Vava disappeared back to Paris and was never seen again.

Another strange event which triggered many long conversations about the past was when Anastasia, the Tsar's youngest daughter, suddenly appeared in Berlin alive and well. A book was published and later a film was made describing her survival from the bullets that had somehow hit the jewels sewn into her corsets and saved her from certain death. This was how she had survived the terrible slaughter of the family in the cellars of the house in Ekaterinburg.

It was reported that she spoke mainly German but knew so many intimate details of their life and all their relations in Tsarskoe Selo, it was hard not to believe. Ida refused to believe a word of it from the beginning. This went on for years and the question of whether or not it was Anastasia made big news. Ida said it was all a big hoax and money making scam but the mystery remained unsolved until the discovery and DNA testing of the royal bones so many years later proved she was right.

The boardinghouse contained many relics from their past and remained completely unchanged as the years went by. 'Governess' and 'Bolshevik' became outdated words as I grew older and better able to understand their conversations. It seemed as though nothing would change. Grandmother's porcelain figurines still stood on the sideboard – delicate moulded figures of two Cossacks in astrakhan hats and fur trimmed jackets – one making a hole in the ice with a long pointed pole, the other fishing through a hole in the ice. The enamelled coronation beaker – dating from 1896 to commemorate the coronation of the Tsar and grandmother's trip to Moscow stood on the kitchen windowsill with the tea caddy picturing two Russian peasants on the lid. The large family portrait taken in Russia when they were young children was never moved from the hallway and grandfather's picture, 'The Thin Red Line', a painting of the battle of Balaclava during the Crimean war hung at the top of the stairs over his bookcase containing whole sets of books in Russian – read and re-read by May.

In May's room two small icons hung over her bed and a jewellery box from Baden Baden stood on her dressing table with the brass nameplate which grandfather had unscrewed from the door of the house next to the Phoenix iron foundry when he left Petersburg in 1906. Strangest of all was the large white ashtray advertising some hotel in Santiago which for as long as I can remember was used as a soap dish in the bathroom – a memory of grandfather's disastrous journey to Chile. There was also a big portrait of grandmother when she was young holding a basket of flowers, smiling, looking down from the dining room wall in an ornate Russian frame.

May sat amongst these relics like Miss Havisham. The carpets grew threadbare, the curtains faded like the wallpaper and May grew very old with her books, memories and ghosts.

It was in 1964 I met Nina Michaelovna on a trip to Leningrad just as the iron curtain was beginning to lift. Mr Krushchev, Russia's new prime minister, had made a visit to America and Russian astronauts were the heroes of the day. It was a time of great optimism. Nina Michaelovna sat by a tall window in a small second floor flat in an old building entered by way of a dark concrete stairwell. The room was filled with dark, heavy furniture and there was a large photograph of a Borzoi dog in profile on one of the walls. It seemed as though I had taken a step back into my mother's youth.

Nina Michaelovna's face was like parchment, small and very wrinkled but still with the black shining eyes I had seen in photographs. I was ushered into a seat next to her in the window space and still refusing to speak any English she held my hand as

Natasha took over the conversation. For most of her young life Natasha had worked in the theatre and cabaret as an actress and dancer. She had married twice and had two daughters, Ninisha and Oxana, who were both very eager to show me around Leningrad. Natasha asked many questions about my mother's life and what they had heard about the affluence of the west. They had none of the consumer goods on show in any of the shops there at that time so it was rather a taboo subject amongst a gathering of communists which they had since become.

The warmth of Nina Michaelovna's hand throughout my visit made a much closer contact than any of the conversation going on in the room. Before I left Ninisha found a very prolific Russian 'penfriend' for me, an English student, Vladimir Pavlovitch, who also escorted me around the sights of Leningrad and with whom I have corresponded ever since. I saw many of the buildings where my mother had been, the Admiralty and the Smolni (once attended by great aunt Adelaide), also the great winter palace of the Tsar's, now the 'Hermitage', a vast museum and art gallery for the people.

Huge idealistic schemes were being pioneered in education and my new friend, the English student, had to spend a whole year of his training in some remote, isolated villages teaching English. 'How petty and futile were all the consumer goods of the capitalist countries compared to this?' he asked. It was all very impressive. My mother made the journey the following year and met Nina Michaelovna, with whom she had kept up a correspondence for almost 50 years. The Russia of her youth had disappeared but she never forgot that summer in Kuokkola or her happy childhood at the house on the Palustrovskaya quay where she was born.

Imagine my surprise to discover one of the last letters written by the Tsarina Alexandra mentions Ida's name and was written from her captivity in Tobolsk to her close friend Anna Verubova, before the family's fatal journey to Ekaterinburg where they were all brutally murdered by the Bolsheviks. In spite of all the horrors of her captivity she still retains her gossipy style of conversation in writing, almost as though Anna was sitting next to her. This letter, probably at a huge cost, was somehow smuggled out of Tobolsk and could have easily been intercepted by the Bolsheviks. She also mentions 'A.P.' (Alexander Pistolkors) and his brother Dmitri, who was exiled to Persia after his involvement in the murder of Rasputin. The Tsarina had demanded that he was to be executed by firing squad but was over-ruled by the Tsar and exiled to Persia. She was quite aware of the fact that Alexander Pistolkors and his side of the family, led by Grand duke Paul and Princess Paley, were very strongly opposed to Rasputin whilst Aylia and Anna Verubova were his devoted followers. Ida and the three children had been in the middle of these two opposing factions so it was little wonder she had refused to go back and join them in Copenhagen. Here is the extract:

'And how is your poor sister Aylia? I hope she is not too sad. She has friends? Her husband? Has he not become too sad away from her? And how are the sweet children? Miss Ida is still with her I hope. How glad I am that you have seen 'A.P.' Did he not seem strange out of uniform? And what did he say about his brother?

Ah, all is past and will never return. We must begin a new life and forget self, my deal little soul.

Christ be with you. Alexandra